MIKE AND DAVE

NEED WEDDING DATES

MIKE and DAVE STANGLE

Pocket Books

New York   London   Toronto   Sydney   New Delhi

Pocket Books
An Imprint of Simon & Schuster, Inc.
1230 Avenue of the Americas
New York, NY 10020

First Pocket Books paperback edition July 2016

POCKET and colophon are registered trademarks of Simon & Schuster, Inc.

For information about special discounts for bulk purchases, please contact Simon & Schuster Special Sales at 1-866-506-1949 or business@simonandschuster.com.

The Simon & Schuster Speakers Bureau can bring authors to your live event. For more information or to book an event, contact the Simon & Schuster Speakers Bureau at 1-866-248-3049 or visit our website at www.simonspeakers.com.

Manufactured in the United States of America

10   9   8   7   6   5   4   3   2   1

ISBN 978-1-5011-4727-2
ISBN 978-1-4767-6010-0 (ebook)

Acknowledgments

To our brother, Sean.
For being our Cooper Manning and sitting this one out.

To our dad, JT Stangle.
You've already read too much. Go back to Bill O'Reilly books.

To our agent, Michelle.
Thanks for finding us, then making our lives *way* cooler.

To our other agent, Cait.
For somehow amplifying all the stuff Michelle did for us.

To our editor, Jeremie.
For trying to read our "C-section" line aloud in a Simon & Schuster staff meeting. You sicko.

To our other editor, Kiele.
Thanks for still talking to us after you read our first draft. And for changing it.

To Jay Barbeau.

Everyone should look Jay up on Facebook and add him as a friend *right now*. Mike will drink a Zima on YouTube for every ten new friends he gets.

To the state of Colorado.

For legalizing grass just as we were about to finish this book, for the third time.

To 1996's "Dancing Baby" viral video.

For going viral first. Though considered adorable at the time, with today's advancements in 3D technology it would surely qualify as baby-porn. Ooga-Chaka!

To Pop Rocks and soda.

For taking internet virality and giving it an unwarranted bad-boy feel.

To *SpaceBalls*.

For basically being the best movie ever.

To Craigslist.

For pulling the ol' *Price-Is-Right* "$1 DOLLAR, BOB!" on eBay. They never saw it coming.

To Dick Cheney.

Because we can say, "Hey man, at least we're not Dick Cheney" when people give us shit about this book, and they'll be all like "you're right." Handshake.

To our friends, so many to name.
You're much funnier than we are. You had a part in
any part of this book that makes our readers laugh. So,
probably seven people have laughed because of you.
Way to help us write a shitty book. Thanks for that.

Sur La Table of Contents

Author's Note

(Dave)

It's difficult to write one book between two people, especially because Mike is borderline illiterate. Still, it's tricky to establish a single voice, and the reader can become confused as to who is talking when. Truth is, it's both of us talking, always, regardless of "whose story" it is. Every chapter is a collaboration between us—written, edited, re-edited, scrapped, started over, argued over, drunk over, and then, finally, shoved by both of us face-first through a plate glass window to the finish line (and always past our deadlines).

If that confuses you, we're sorry. Now you know how Mike feels all the time.

Preface

A Letter to Our Mother, Denise

Dear Mom,

You look great today. Have you done something different with your hair? We love it! Not a lot of women can pull off that look. Good for you.

Mama, we've been asked to write a book and unfortunately, it's mostly the stuff we promised we'd never tell you. Like—remember a few years back when you made us breakfast as we recapped that crazy Christmas party? You finally asked us to stop when Dave said, "You'd be surprised how realistic the vagina felt!" You laughed and you cried and you made us promise never to repeat that story in front of Dad. This book is like that, but *way* worse.

For as long as we can remember, you've led by example and taught us what is important to enjoy and what is important to forget. You taught us not to take ourselves too seriously. You taught us what pairs best with wine (more wine, so simple). Dad may think we're complete degenerates, and you might not always want to hear the details, but we know that deep down, you're glad we're having fun.

Come to think of it, just skip the damn book and let's go have some wine.

We love you,
Mike and Dave

Dave and Mike, after a very high FaceTime brotherly catch-up/ pump-up.
December 18, 2013.

Introduction

Meet the Stangles!

(Dave)

Oh man, first off—the book cover reveals our full names, and when our dad reads what's in here, he is going to shit himself. He will actually shit, and if he is wearing pants at the time, he will shit *himself*. He wants nothing to do with any of this "nonsense." When he first heard we were writing a book, he requested final editorial approval on the entire thing. Oh hey Dad, are you NUTS? We aren't writing a book on conservative talk radio or upstate New York's best driving roads.

Republican. Robust mustache. Wise. Old. Duck farts. Disapproval. Tough love: John Stangle. You can't blame our dad for not being crazy about all of this. He's old-school. He is the face of old-school. You could even argue his appearance resembles that of an actual old school. It needs restoration, funding is tight, and it just wasn't designed to handle this many kids! Besides, his political beliefs don't allow room in the budget for excess government spending. Johnny could never have predicted that his future wife's wild side was genetic, destined to dominate his boring, by-the-book, law-abiding genes when drawing up the Punnett squares for the Stangle kids. John Thomas Stangle (JT) was born in the same village in which he still currently resides, sixty-two years later. Yes, we're from a village. It's the same village where our entire family was born and raised. How many people do you know who grew up in a village, and aren't either an Eskimo or a Smurf? Well, now you know two, and you're about to meet a few more. The Village of Menands was founded in 1924, and as of the 2010 census, the population was just shy of four thousand people (we'll get there, just wait for 2020!). Our dad loves Menands; it's a part of everything that is JT Stangle. He even currently holds the title of "Village Clerk," just so nothing goes on within village lines that he doesn't have some sort of scent of in that old hound dog nose of his. Old-school guys like our dad are often labeled as hard-asses. He is a hard-ass, but it's also important to know he is a really sweet fella. Like Jeff Bridges's character in *True Grit,* he is a likable, stand-up, grizzled old soul of a hard-ass whom you root for. That's our old man. No wonder he's been able to lock up a dime like our mom since '74.

Our mom, Denise, (Denny, to her friends) didn't grow up far from Menands. She was only a few towns away, actually. You know what's cool about our folks? They are high school sweethearts. From villages. I know! God, they're cute. They've been married forty years. Cheers, you two. They met when they were seventeen. Denny claims that my dad is the only guy she has banged throughout her entire life, but we don't buy it. Come on,

Mom! If that's the case, you missed out, even for that day and age. In any case, we're happy to say that, somehow, JT and Denny are still smitten to this day. Denise is the very definition of "Forever Young." Rod Stewart might have even written the song about her. Did he write that song? He certainly sang it; he sang the *shit* out of it.

Denny encompasses so many incredibly admirable character traits, Mike and I would be lucky to inherit half of them between us. Denny is intrinsically kind, selfless, and caring. She is wildly patient, wise, and has seen it all. She is a great cook, makes a mean cocktail, and can even fix a zipper! She is like a professional mom, but being a friend is her passion. Denny is the complete package. If you didn't pick up on this already, Mike and I aren't ashamed to admit we're huge mama's boys. I'm proud of it. With a mama like this, who wouldn't be a mama's boy? Denny is the throbbing heart of our big old family.

And she raised four kids! Oh yeah, Mike and I aren't the only ones. Did we mention that? Two came before us; we're numbers three and four. If there are a couple of fractions somewhere out there in between us, JT, we won't hold it against you. The seventies were a wild time. The chronological leader of the pack is our brother Sean, age thirty-five. He's a real tool. Whether or not we actually believe that is known only to us. Sorry, Sean, when two brothers write a book without the remaining brother, they're compelled to take advantage of the opportunity and call the third brother a tool in print. Sean lives in

Las Vegas, Nevada. The day after Sean graduated from college, his long-term girlfriend dumped him (ha!), so he packed up and moved out to Vegas with a few buddies on a whim. Power move. They all still live out there to this day. Sean has two degrees—one in mathematics and another in some sort of engineering. What's he do out there for a living? Oh, he's a bartender. In Vegas, he's a "mixologist," if you ask him. He pours different combinations of liquor over ice and serves it to bachelor parties, businessmen, and entertainers until they work up the courage to go spend a night with hookers. But he is a damn fine mixologist. Sean knows more about booze and hospitality than anyone I've ever met.

For us, this is both a blessing and a curse. It takes a real sick son of a bitch to actually be able to *survive* while living in Vegas. Think about that for a second. Most normal humans have a firm two-night, three-day limit in Vegas before they lose it. Personally, if I'm within Vegas city limits for more than thirty-six hours, I turn into Teen Wolf and start surfing tops of moving vans. Sean is different. I used to think he was the smart one, but that was just because Mike and I have been acting like idiots the last fifteen years. Our cat, Sticky, seemed smart compared to us, and he was literally diagnosed as "a retarded cat." That's the vet's phrase, not ours.

My parents didn't put up with nearly as much shit from Sean as they did from us. Sean had to go through the first-time-parent shit. When Sean was seventeen, he wasn't allowed to ride in the car with other high school kids, because it "was dangerous." Things loosened up so much for me that by the time I was seventeen, I was paying twelve-year-olds to chauffeur me around! Hell— by the time Mike was seventeen, he got arrested for throwing a giant party on the roof of our middle school, a story that would appear on the local news. No wonder Sean lives in Vegas now; he's making up for lost time. Now is also a good opportunity to mention that Sean is only six feet tall, while we rose to the handsome height of six four (though Mike claims to be six five).

Then there's Kristen. She's the only girl and is 100 percent our old man's favorite. She always has been. Kristen is like the Vlad Putin of Stangle offspring sibling popularity. She runs unopposed, every term. She is also an absolute character. We've never met anyone more comfortable, aware, and honest about who she is. Kristen does exactly what she feels like doing all the time. If she wants something, she buys it. If she wants to go somewhere, she goes there. If she doesn't want to be somewhere, she leaves. She is incredibly unfiltered. She's a tough cookie, too; she had to be, after growing up surrounded by three brothers. That poor girl couldn't bring a prospective guy near the house without us turning into a bunch of junkyard Rottweilers. Her first boyfriend was this turd named Jay. He worked at a Pokémon/Magic: The Gathering trading card store in the mall. The kid had a chin-strap beard at eighteen years old. Jay also went to our rival high school: South Colonie, the Garnet Raiders! We Stangle boys could read the writing on the wall that Jay was bad news. With an effort spearheaded by JT himself, we brothers tried to shake Kristen's young love for this dirtbag. We tried everything! When Kris and Jay would sneak off to start Frenching somewhere, Sean and I would send Mike in there, ten years old and armed with a spatula, to break up the lip wrestling. But no matter how many times we tried, we learned that Kristen cannot be deterred. If she wants it—she gets it.

Now you're starting to get the complete Stangle family picture. JT and Denny, Sean and Kris, then the shithead duo of Mike and myself. The first time we described ourselves to the public, we didn't know it would be public at all. We were just fucking around. It provided a fun, creative outlet to break up the day. Had we known one of our Craigslist posts would go viral and be read by so many people, we might have put a little more thought into it.

Who Is Dave Stangle?

Dave and Frank, both seemingly unimpressed.

(Mike)

Meet my big brother Dave: Division One athlete, business professional, grade-A scumbag. Dave is my mother's favorite. Why? Good fucking question. We're talking about the guy who out of sheer boredom spent all of this past Christmas Eve trying to convince my father of his made-up-on-the-spot homosexuality. The guy who dressed up like a stray dog for Halloween only so he could bark and growl loudly at women and piss, dick out and leg up, on every fire hydrant he passed in Manhattan. The guy who insists on pulling his pants (and underpants) all the way down every time he pees in a public urinal—affection-ately referring to this as "the preschool pee-pee." I real-ize I sound bitter here, but it's just unbridled jealousy. My big brother is an inspiration: perverse lunatic meets brilliant, charismatic piece of shit. He is creative, ballsy, and has no—absolutely, positively *no*—conscience what-soever. It's a lethal combination.

People who don't know him typically assume he makes up most of his stories, but I've been an eyewitness to more than I'd care to admit, and in most cases he's ac-tually toning it down. Dave has been punched in the dick by a midget! He was once roundhouse kicked in the face by a female all-American kung fu master (he would kill me if I didn't make sure to mention that he ended up winning that fight "unanimously," even though it took place on our front lawn). I might hate him 51 percent of the time and love him the other 49 percent, but I'd be lying if I didn't admit he's the perfect guy to have in your corner 100 per-cent of the time, even if he has the most fucked-up priori-ties of all time. In a pinch and need a condom? Don't go to Dave in a million years. Need an iPhone 5 charger? He's got six in his top drawer, where the condoms should be.

I am not a writer and I don't pretend to be, but I'm not even sure Dave can put together a grammatically sound sentence. Seriously, the hardest part of writing this whole thing has been correcting his use of "there," "their," and "they're." Dave, how do you even survive professionally? At the end of the day, my brother and I have a lot in common, but I think what makes us most similar is that we've both always believed that to survive as modern-day young gentlemen, we need to have as much fun as possible while giving as few fucks about as few things as possible. We want the last check we write to bounce. I'm lucky to have Dave, this big ol' mess, as my older brother, making all the mistakes I never had to make, treading through all the mud while my shoes stayed white.

Okay, Dave, me now me now.

Wait, Who Is Mike Stangle?

Here we see Mike, stoned.

(Dave)

Mike Stangle isn't just a complete accident that resulted from a road trip our folks took back in 1987. Back then, my mom and dad drove counterclockwise around the outer border of the United States in my dad's gray panel van (one of *several* full-size vans my dad has owned in his lifetime). It didn't have any chairs or benches in the back, you know, 'cause it was a fucking panel van. Our old man just heaved a mattress back there so he and my mom could save on hotel costs. What a classic move! I honestly don't know how you *don't* get a chick pregnant with that plan, but as far as I could tell, no one knew what the hell was going on in the eighties, anyway. Thousands of miles and several dozen boxes of wine later, Mike was conceived. Ew!

Since then, Mike has been sucking up one-quarter of my parents' attention that otherwise would have been nicely allocated three ways between my brother, sister, and me. *I* was supposed to be the baby, the family caboose! Instead, I spent my childhood in the middle with my sister. In the meantime, Mike got away with all the shit I got in trouble for. My parents were so worried about the things my buddies and I were up to that they forgot to worry about Mike. The youngest always grows up fast. I'm pretty sure he knew how to put on a rubber before I did. Mike has been a grade-A sexual deviant from a very young age; he figured things out quicker than most kids. The first time I ever put a condom on, I thought that it was supposed to go around my balls, too. Turns out that is basically impossible. The condoms just kept snapping as I stretched them around my entire dick and balls, then they would go flying off like popped balloons, twirling around the room and making the dog bark.

Mike is *constantly* approached by gay men looking for a good time, despite his (allegedly) unwavering love for females. The top-line fact is that Mike has lived his youth in a way that, upon reflection, splits grown men into two camps. In the first camp are the men who see Mike and regret their own comparatively tame youth. But if they're lucky, they're in the second camp—those who look at Mike and are reminded immediately of just how much they truly nailed it. Mike is so many things: unemployed nomad, string cheese enthusiast, scooter rider, silly heart, currently sweating in a men's room john. I could go on and on. At this point, I'm just riding his coattails; there is no possible way I can keep up. I may be one sick pup, but Mike is a different breed altogether. Have you ever woken up on an Indian reservation? In Canada? Mike has. Try to figure that one out. We're talking about a guy who once accidentally drank his own semen. Fact. He's the guy who got so drunk before we went on *Anderson Cooper* (films at 11 a.m. on a Tuesday, mind you) that he couldn't remember what state Orlando was in. He has a knack for three things: overeating, armpit sweat, and finding adventure everywhere he sets foot. Yes, two of those are serious flaws that keep him from romantic success. But he's not all dick jokes and frat stories; never mind that he was never even in a frat and that he has a terrible dick (both true).

We aren't womanizers. We aren't frat boys. We aren't even that weird or fucked-up. We just say yes a lot. Strange things happen when you let your guard down.

You've got to be successful to write a how-to, and you've got to be helpful to write a self-help book—we're neither of these things. But we do know what it feels like to let our freak flags fly. So, if you have a son, give this to him when he graduates from college; he'll relate. If you have a daughter, what's up with her? Is she around?

A Media Tour Done Right

Lauer, Coops, and the Gang

(Dave)

We'd been putting stupid shit on Craigslist for years. If you live in New York, you use Craigslist to get shit done or to rent a shitty apartment because you're always poor. We used Craigslist to fuck around. That Craigslist wedding ad that somehow went viral? I wrote that on the notes section of my iPhone while taking a number two in the men's room at work. It took approximately one poop to write. I pasted it into an email to Mike, he added all the parts I couldn't (I had to wipe) and corrected my absolutely horrible grammar, then *boom*—up on the Net. It was up for about a week, and the results were pretty stagnant. We sent it around to our buddies for some cheap laughs, then figured we could get some really entertaining responses—you know, the types of responses you expect from the *totally normal crowd* cruising Craigslist on a regular basis. It took one tweet from a friend with a sizeable Twitter following (hey Starky!) and we were off! But it snowballed like a motherfucker. It went from Reddit to Buzzfeed to Gawker to *New York* magazine to the *Huffington Post*! It was everywhere, and it was awesome:

Two Fellas Need Wedding Dates

From our Craigslist ad.
Everything in this picture makes so much sense.

My brother and I are looking for wedding dates for our cousin's wedding in majestic Saratoga, New York, on March 23rd, 2013.

We've been told by the bride that bringing dates is "mandatory" so we "won't harass all of my friends all night" and "stay under control." Rather than ask some fringe women in our lives to go and face the inevitable "does this mean he wants to take it to the next level!?" questions, we'd rather bring complete strangers and just figure it out. Still reading? In anticipation of your questions we've developed an FAQ section below.

Dave, Mike . . . What's in it for me?

- An excuse to get dressed up

- Open bar & food all night

- Eccentric/downright dangerous bro-2-bro dance moves (may need to sign a waiver)

- Adventure

- Mystery

- Suspense

- True Love

- Royalties once our night's story is developed into a romantic comedy*

*if this happens (we estimate the chances at 85 percent) we refuse to let Ashton Kutcher play either of our characters, however, we will consider him for a supporting role.

SO—What are you fellas like, anyway?

Oh us? We're both in our 20s, single, dashingly tall, Anglo-Saxon, respectfully athletic, love to party, completely house trained, relaxed, passionate, smell great, have cool hair, clean up nice, boast great tie collections, will promise to shave, love our mother, have seen *Love Actually* several times, controversial, provocative, short-sighted (with a big picture mentality), raw, emotional, sensitive, but still bad boys.

What should us ladies be like?

You should respond in pairs as you'll want to know at least 1 person at this wedding. Sisters (twins?!) are preferable, but we'll take friends, or even enemies. You should be attractive or our aunts will judge you, but not TOO attractive or one of our uncles might grope you. You should be relaxed and easy going as we'll probably make up flattering lies about you on the spot. You should own a dress, or be able to acquire one because we don't have any. If (when) you respond you should send some pictures of yourself so we know you've met the above re-quirements. Feel free to include a resume; this is a classy wedding and we're looking for well-rounded women. Interesting/unique pairings are encouraged; don't be afraid to make yourself stand out!

This feels kinda creepy, are you guys Craigslist killers?

No. Well, if you want to be techni . . . nevermind. No, we aren't. We just genuinely want to do something different and we don't see any other way to approach it. What would verify our normalness? Facebook? Instagram? We can have a pre-date screening (interview) prior to the wedding and play 20 questions over a coupla cocktails if you'd like?

We're IN! What now?

First off—smart thinking. Email us, send along some pictures, information, high school athletic stats, questions, etc. We'll take it from there.

• • •

We were getting blown the fuck *up*. I'd get up from my desk for two minutes to take a leak, and I'd come back to 254 new responses from 508 babes (they applied in pairs, it's simple babe math). What's more is we had responses from the press—reporters, bloggers, journalists, and even this complete *bitch* from our hometown newspaper, the *Times Union*! Her name is Kristy Barlette for the record.

For at least the first few days, we replied to every single email. Some were babes, some were not-so-babes, some were old ladies, some were dudes, some were dudes saying they wish they'd thought of this. Gals submitted pictures, PowerPoints, videos, blogs, even some nudie shots! Soon ABC and NBC were competing to do stories on us. Naturally, we pitted them against each other to get the most bang for our buck. It worked. It became a national story. In a matter of days, we went from typing on our iPhones while taking a dump to accepting invitations to nationally televised interviews. What the fuck is the matter with you, America?

Our first stop was with NBC on the *Today* show. Some folks from NBC's *Dateline* division were working on a story about us for a show that was set to air later that summer. Guess who the host was? Chris Hansen from *To Catch a Predator*. Ha! That guy certainly loves his perverts. What a perfect fit! The entire NBC special on us eventually ended up falling through. After a few weeks of Mike and me pushing off the corny narrative NBC was trying to create (so much for "news"), we gave Kim the *Dateline* producer a nervous breakdown. She said we drank too much and weren't "fit for the camera" and "take this seriously" and "You *have* to wear shirts." We got some mileage out of it before it fell apart. To push the story's development further, Kim got us booked on *Today,* and for the Monday morning after the Oscars, no less. The *Today* show is composed of 80 percent fluff, 15 percent news, and 5 percent Carson Daly somehow still sticking around. That means the day after the Oscars is one of their most-viewed broadcasts of the year. There would be a lot of eyeballs on us, Kim said. We should make sure to be ourselves. You got it, Kim! I distinctly remember the exact conversation Mike and I had the night before. We weren't going to try to be funny, we weren't going to bend to producers trying to make a good story, we weren't going to say what we were supposed to say or put any effort into coming off as likable. Instead, we were going to act exactly as we had for years: drunk and confused as to why we were there.

Our segment was slated for around 9:30 a.m. that Monday, so Kim arranged for a car to come scoop us up at 7 a.m. She really stressed that she would prefer us not to drink the night before, fearing we'd sleep in and look like shit. No problem, Kim. We'll just get up at 4:30 a.m. to start drinking instead. I don't care who you are, you don't go on the *Today* show sober.

At the time, I was really into making French pressed coffee. I was fucking around with these mint coffee beans that were an absolute delight. You know what makes a big cup of mint iced coffee even better? When 50 percent of it is bourbon, that's what. It was 4:45 a.m. on a Monday morning, and Mike and I and Frank the bulldog were blasting my only Pandora station at the time—*Summer Hits of the 90s*—while throwing back spiked iced coffees at an alarming rate. By the time our car arrived, we were pretty tuned up. We'd done at least two hundred push-ups each, changed our outfits nearly as many times, and were ready to roll. The fun part about drinking this way is that the alcohol has been amplified by at least seven cups of coffee, so your body is really partying. Spiked iced coffees are the Red Bull and vodka of the morning.

By the time we got to 30 Rock and found Denny, made it through security, ran into Michael Phelps, and sat down in the greenroom, we were legitimately wasted. You want to talk about a fucking *dork*? Let's talk about

Michael Phelps. You'd think a twenty-two-time Olympic medalist would get some amusement from two drunk strangers trying to engage him in a debate over what the *best* five-dollar foot-long is. Mike was pushing meatball marinara (such a slob) over my classic cold-cut combo. I can't believe Phelps didn't back me up. He was sitting in the middle of our heated debate and acted like we didn't exist. Screw you, Phelps! Lochte 2016!!!

Before it came time to hit the *Today* show couch, we were introduced to Natalie Morales (babe) and Matt Lauer (*super*babe!). I basically shoved Natalie aside to shake hands with Matt. I couldn't even tell you what Natalie looked like, but I can recall in detail exactly how nice Matt's suit was. He was fit as a fiddle, too. And his handshake? Top-notch. We exchanged pleasantries for a few minutes, until they realized that it was indeed a gallon of bourbon they smelled on our breath.

As they finished another segment, we got mic'd up on the couch. We noticed a set of thick-rim glasses and an iPhone on the coffee table in front of Matt's chair. Lauer, you fool! Mike and I wasted no time. We posed for selfies on his phone until Lauer came in from his segment. He wasn't happy with us. He made that clear. That was when we saw a true dose of Lauer Power. He calmly sat down in his chair, informed us we had one minute and thirty seconds until we were on, then began to rip us apart. For a minute and twenty-nine seconds straight, he attacked everything about us—our suits, how goofy we were, Mike's sweat issues, my boner that wouldn't go away, grammatical errors in our Craigslist ad (my fault), where this amount of bourbon consumption would probably lead us long term, you name it. I've never respected a man more. This was a guy who interviewed Barack Obama two weeks earlier and came off as the most articulate journalist in the country. Now he was slicing and dicing two drunk goons on his couch. The second the cameras turned to us, he snapped right back into business mode. Total pro.

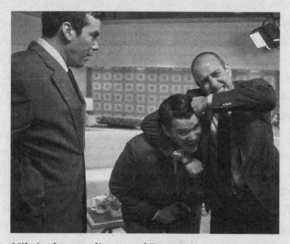

Mike's close to climax and Dave is in active orgasm.
They really like Matt Lauer. *Photo courtesy of Denise Stangle*

The next stop on our media tour took place a few days later. You think my man-crush on Lauer was big? Let's talk about Anderson Cooper. Whenever I need to do a gay litmus test on myself (every couple of months), I stare at a picture of Coops for an hour straight. In the end, if my wiener doesn't move, it confirms I'm not gay. Bottom line: if I can't be attracted to that man, I can't be attracted to any man. How does he get his hair to look like that? It doesn't even make sense.

Needless to say, when Mike and I found out we were going on Coops, we were ecstatic. We again woke up at 4:30 a.m. to start partying, put down a dozen bourbon mint coffees, and listen to *Summer Hits of the 90s*, because why the fuck wouldn't we? Except this time we had guests. The night before we had gone on a double date with two gals who replied to our Craigslist ad, and wouldn't ya know, it turned into a double sleepover. The ladies were understandably alarmed when Mike and I started pacing around the apartment ass-naked, doing push-ups.

We four lovebirds piled into the car service SUV at 10:30 a.m. and headed toward Coops's studio. We were all over the girls, making out, touchin' boobies, actin' a fool! You'd think our driver would be horrified. Nope. Not Sal. Guys named Sal are incapable of being horrified. I might name my son Sal.

Those gals were swell, but they weren't so thrilled when we got to the studio and their names weren't on the security list. It was the perfect out; security had done our dirty work. Before departing, Mike grabbed his gal by both sides of her face and gave her this really long, passionate, and awkward kiss goodbye. It sounded like he was trying to suck a kiwi out of its skin. It was at this point I began to realize how much drunker he was than me. When Mike is really drunk, he takes long pauses in an effort to come off like he is thinking. Usually in this time, he forgets the answer, the question, who he is talking to, and where he is. I could see him doing this as the producer for Coops's show was briefing us. She hated us immediately. This made me ecstatic. We were the least popular guys in the building, but we were having the most fun. By the time we got to the greenroom, Mike's coordination was on the level of a newborn fawn with Down syndrome. I took over making the cocktails—I wasn't going to risk him spilling the bourbon. *Make it easy on me,* he slurred to me. What? *Give yourshelf more bourbon than . . . I do.* I made him a mixture composed of 70 percent bourbon, 20 percent coffee, and 10 percent sweetener, so it'd go down real nice. That's what big brothers are for.

Before we went on set, we once again headed over to get our makeup done. This time, I found myself making small talk with Honey Boo Boo and her giant mother—Mama June. I told them I loved their show and asked if they had any extra "go-go juice" for me. But—fun fact—they were not at all Honey Boo Boo or Mama June. I was completely mistaken. I can't decide what is more offensive—having a guy mistake your daughter for Honey Boo Boo or being mistaken for Mama June. Awkward. I tried to bring up the five-dollar foot-long debate, but it just didn't play.

On Coops's show there are three rows in front that are reserved for guests. During each commercial break, the next guest will move one row closer to the front, which is in the same lens shot as Coops himself. But Mike and I sat down front and center and refused to move, even though we weren't slated to be on for forty minutes. This means that every guest before us had to do their segment sandwiched between two lumbering giants. In fact, we were so close to their microphones that we could weigh in on everything. Blackout Mike began to peak. He'd squeeze in a random thought or affirmation, despite having no idea what anyone was talking about.

Our segment with Coops couldn't have gone better! Did we look very drunk? Yes. Did I tune out his first question because I couldn't wait to say *Thanks for having us on, Coops. You look fantastic today as always?* You fucking know it. We were happy to get a lot of good laughs out of the audience. However, our ultimate goal was to give a secret "shout-out" to our friends during the interview. Mike and I had decided on a code word—"Orlando, Florida." I don't know why we went with "Orlando, Florida," you guys, we just did. To be honest, I was so caught up with the interview that I had forgotten about the plan. But when Coops asked where our wedding date applications were coming from, Mike perked up. He looked like Bernie from *Weekend at Bernie's II*. Fourteen seconds later, a big grin appeared on his face and he said, "Oh . . . rlando." Another five seconds to add ". . . Florida!" The guys got their shout-out, Coops gave us an *are you guys actually retarded?* look, and the bit came to an end. Everyone seemed pretty pleased, except the producer.

She had security escort us out of the building *immediately* after our segment was over. Coops declined both an invitation to the wedding and our request for a friendly photograph. He must have been pretty busy. Nationally televised interview number two was a great success.

The third stop was probably our favorite—the Australian TV show also known as *Today,* which is broadcast on the Nine Network. Jackpot. Mike and I have always gotten along well with Australians. We're cut from very similar cloth. Mike even lived in Australia for a while and then refused to come home. He ran away to Fiji with an Aussie gal he met while he was over there. Our parents freaked out, but I knew something had to give—she was *way* out of his league. The *Today* show in Australia was right in our wheelhouse. Australians are like Americans, except *all* of them are cool, instead of just some of them. With Lauer Power and Coops, we got drunk to stand out and go against the grain, but for *Today* in Australia, we were getting blasted just to blend in. They scheduled our interview at three in the afternoon on St. Patrick's Day. Hello! We didn't even have to get up early, but we still did. Four thirty a.m. worked so well for us the first few times that we decided to stick with it. When we arrived at the studio, we were one level less than "Coops drunk," but we had also smoked a whole bunch of grass on our walk there. We were making jokes that only the two of us found funny. Luckily, it never became an issue, because the studio only had one guy, and he wasn't even Australian! He was just a dude named Kirk.

Kirk set up everything for us to do a live feed to Australia. Then he noticed we were drunk and directed us toward the extensive liquor cabinet. We all immediately became best friends. Frank the bulldog was with us, too. He wanted a taste of the action, and Kirk didn't seem to mind at all. Frank ate a bunch of popcorn while Kirk, Mike, and I sat around the studio kitchen drinking warm bourbon and smoking grass out of various pieces of fruit from a gourmet basket sent to the studio by one of my personal favorite Australians—Kylie Minogue. She is such a babe. Oh, by the way, the fruit was dipped in truffle-salted chocolate. Talk about high class. In my life, I've never felt finer smoking grass out of a piece of fruit.

Eventually, we took the call from Cameron Williams, the host. Cam was smooth as silk. The best part about the Australian *Today* interview was that Frank was walking on and off the set periodically, sniffing things and humping the leg of the stool Mike was sitting on. No one said a single thing. Kirk didn't intervene or motion for us to get him to stop; Cam didn't even acknowledge him. It was as if two drunk guys and a troublemaking, butt-sniffing junkyard dog were par for the course in every Australian's morning.

Our Own
Personal eHarmony

(Mike)

Online dating is here to stay, whether we like it or not. From now on, it will be part of every young person's social and love life. Except Dave's. Or mine. To this day, neither one of us has gone on an actual date with someone we've met through online dating. Of course, that doesn't mean we don't dabble. We'd never pass up an opportunity for awkward exchanges with so many members of the opposite sex. Take a few minutes to consider the niche markets that have developed for all the weirdos out there. It goes to show that there really is someone for everyone. If you're hoping that mustlovevampires.com helps you find the future Mrs. You, something is probably a little off . . . but at least you know that will also be the case for whomever you get matched with, too! Have you guys seen the online dating websites out there these days?

FarmersOnly.com
For farmers, *only*.

YouMustLoveDogsDating.com
Their dogs can watch *them* hump, for a change.

Vampiresonly.com
For Goth kids who all of a sudden aren't feeling so hopeless after all.

Tinder
For sluts.

Catpeople.com
Made that one up, but I guarantee it exists in some form, though.

Dave discovered these sites last year the week after he spent the entire Thanksgiving break refurbishing this early-twentieth-century wooden trunk he found in our parents' attic. He was out in our garage for hours every day buffing this thing, sanding it, staining it, all that shit. It came out awesome. But the combination of fumes, metal particles, and dust ended up making Dave deathly ill, and he had to take a few days off work. But Dave doesn't do well when he has to sit still. So instead of recuperating, he spent over seven hours creating a fake online dating profile for me on every major, minor, bizarre, and fucked-up dating website there is. He custom-tailored each profile to be different and to fit the mold of whatever that site's fetish or theme was. He had a different, wildly authentic character, name, and set of pictures for all of them. He had a mission: he wanted to drive responses. Nobody wants to go on a date with a *fake* farmer. The only problem was that you could tell toward the end he started to get lazy. My BlackPeopleMeet.com profile was basically a picture of me where my skin was tinted dark and dreadlocks were Photoshopped onto my head. Also, my face wasn't even on my shoulders, it was free-floating in front of a Jamaican flag. I'm not even going to mention the name he gave me. Horrible. But guess how many hits that got before site administrators took it down? Three! They were big girls.

For at least the next three weeks, we were spending all our free time creating online dating profiles and making sure to use each other's real contact information. Dave's widow's peak and milky white skin already make him look like a vampire, so that one was pretty easy. I also signed him up for this one dating site for people who like to puke on each other. That is the one he never talks about. I secretly think he met up with someone from it and found that he liked it. Officially, though? Neither one of us had ever been on an online date. We were waiting for the right place, the right time, and still figuring out how not to be such pussies. Basically, like so many guys, we wanted it to simply fall into our laps.

When our Craigslist ad went viral, it was like God and Craig teamed up to create a custom online dating website just for us. It was free and received more attention than we ever could have wanted. The timing of it all was perfect, too. Dave and I were both single, working desk jobs in Washington, D.C., and New York, respectively, and suddenly had a fucking Rolodex of women who thought we were way cooler than we actually were. The ad first picked up steam in New York, so I did what any sensible young professional would do. I immediately left for an inordinately long vacation and headed north to Manhattan. I slept on Dave's floor for a solid month. During that month, I was bitten by every insect in the tri-state area. One night, I had to make love with my shirt *on,* because I had so many bites on my back and chest. The takeaway here is that Dave's floor was just filthy. Even after I made a fort out of bedsheets and thumbtacks, I could never hope to call it a home.

The icing on the Craigslist cake was that we were a package deal. That meant every date was a double date. It was like *Double Dare* with Marc Summers, except boobs poured over our heads instead of green slime. Before that, neither one of us had been big daters. These dates, though, they were an experience. For very silly reasons, women were knocking down our door to meet us. What an opportunity. We went on twenty different double dates in the span of twenty-one days. And since I was on a "work hiatus," Dave was forced to pick up the entire tab. The dates were crazy. We didn't quite do our due diligence, but we did use Facebook. It was integral in our formula to select a date for that night:

1. Add the gals as friends.

2. Click on their profile, then on "Photos."

3. Browse through albums and look for key phrases such as "Spring Break," "Summer Lovin'," "Summer Dayz," "Summer 2011," "Summer 2012," "Summer 2013," or "Me and my bitches."

4. Look at every bikini picture available. Pass harsh judgment. Find the hard bodies.

Unsurprisingly, this incredibly shallow vetting process did not result in normal dates. We picked a *lot* of psychos. Most of them were legitimately "run for the fucking hills" types, and we translated that into "drink your way through it, then run for the bedroom." But they were *all* babes. We weren't going on these dates to find love. We wanted to get weird and maybe have a couple of 'gasms along the way. It was mostly about entertainment and pushing it as far as we could every night. Dave began telling the girls about our childhood and how we grew up, except he was completely deadpan explaining that we were interracial adopted brothers who were also cops with a penchant for robbing New York City subway cars. He was essentially reciting the plot of the movie *Money Train,* without anyone catching on. When we would get *really* messed up, one of us would find it hilarious to call dibs on one gal while her friend was within earshot. That move never worked out for anyone, but it did make us laugh.

Double Datin'.

We went to the same exact bar on every single date: Whiskey Town. It was close to Dave's apartment, we knew the fellas in charge, and there was a back door that was perfect for Irish exits. More often than not, there was a Beautiful Girl and her Okay Friend. I think Okay was out there looking for Mr. Right and having no luck, so Okay's mom emailed her our ad after watching the *Today* show. Okay took it as a sign and put together a creative response, then convinced her hottest friend to let her slap some Facebook photos in the response. And it worked, too. Dave loved calling dibs on the hot one. My response to this cheap shot usually depended on my level of intoxication. If I was in decent shape, I'd act offended in front of the gals, appalled at Dave's dick move. If I was drunk enough to be jealous, I'd spend the rest of the night trying to sabotage him until the girls were disgusted enough to leave.

We had only one date that went so terribly that we had to bail midway. We just couldn't handle it. The Okay gal was absolutely nuts, and her hot friend wasn't far behind. Okay gal actually started *eating* the flowers I brought her (flowers are my calling card—Dave's is keeping his socks on during sex). We snuck out when they went to the bathroom to freshen up. When we got a few blocks away, we stopped under some scaffolding to discuss just how crazy Okay gal was. Suddenly, she came sprinting out of *nowhere* and grabbed Dave like a spider monkey! I couldn't believe what I was seeing. Next thing I know, Dave is screaming, "Get it off me, get it off me!" and the girl is wrapped around him with her head *up and inside of his shirt*. He finally pushes her down his legs and off his body, but she is really holding on. Without warning, she sprints off into the night screaming *"I need to see you die!"* For a while, Dave and I just stared at each other. Dave lifted up his shirt to check out the damage to his chest. She had bitten him right between the nipples. I didn't know there was enough skin there to bite on to, but she'd done it. I could see her incisor imprints. We called it a night.

We were starting to notice some issues with our version of "online dating." These girls weren't looking for love or companionship; they were looking for publicity, sex, free drinks, and a story to tell their girlfriends at their next bottomless mimosa brunch. After the chest-biter, we started to prep a little more.

We would hit Whiskey Town early, much earlier than we told the gals to meet us there, because we had learned to get a little destroyed predate. One night, I swear the girls were juniors in college (but read at a senior level). We decided not to ID them—we're not cops, okay? They had gained entry into the bar, and that was good enough by us. They were *college hot*. They were the type of girls who would not have given us the time of day back in school. They were even too hot for us with the older-guy card in play. We did have something, though, and they were here for a reason: we had quickly fading Internet popularity and the good sense to exploit it.

Love was in the air at Whiskey Town that night. The simple and ever-reliable formula of bourbon, slim-fit shirts, and smooth talk was all it took. Even my excessive armpit sweat didn't deter them. The four of us were crushing drinks, snapping selfies, shooting suggestive glances. Our sobriety wasn't helped by the arrival of our friend Anthony, who had a house account for shots. Soon Dave started in on a shtick that became way too familiar in the coming weeks. He drunkenly explained that we needed to go to our place to let his adorable bulldog out to poop. Hook, line, and sinker—Frank, you old son of a bitch! I realized this wasn't Dave's first rodeo using Frank as his wingman-in-waiting.

We all agreed to finish our drinks and head toward Dave's apartment. *Cheers! To Frank!* Exactly ten seconds later, a few bouncers came over and caught us singing "Closing Time" into the security walkie-talkie we had stolen earlier. Apparently they had been scouring the bar trying to figure out which dickheads had taken it. We weren't even really hiding it, hadn't moved from our booth the whole night, and we have very conspicuous singing voices, so the joke was really on them.

On the way home, we walked by our buddy Jay's apartment. He had a second-floor apartment that sat above a storefront with a fire escape hanging right over the street. One of our female companions happened to be a Division One cheerleader and all-around badass. Dave and I promptly convinced her to let us boost her up to the fire escape, so that she could break in and scare our friend Jay. We really wanted to see how Jay would react to a sultry five-foot blond cat burglar breaking into his place. Would he attack her? Would he run? Would he get a little boner? Time would tell. Dave and I warmed up thoroughly, in preparation of collectively lifting ninety-five pounds over our heads. Her friend prepared to film the whole thing for a Vine post later on. These girls were typical college. We had learned earlier that they were going through a phase where they thought it was *hilarious* to talk in Australian accents all the time. The novelty wore off quickly, but it did make her commentary on the resulting video pretty incredible. Anthony had followed us home in a classic fifth-wheel move, and he was unsuccessful in talking us out of boosting her up. She was wearing a short skirt and Dave was staring straight up it. But I wasn't, just so you guys know. She used our boost to do a triple-cork front flip up onto the fire escape, piece of cake! After a quick bow to the crowd that had formed on the street around us, she walked over to the window to pop on in. It was locked. Shit. The jig was up!

The small crowd let out a disappointed sigh and started to dissipate. The only thing left to do was for Alex to gracefully hang off the ledge and fall delicately into our capable, waiting arms. It would've been a lot less expensive if that had been the way things went down. Dave and I stood with arms linked in textbook base-cheerleader form, waiting to catch Alex. This girl is a collegiate athlete and gets thrown in the air and spins all over the place, too. This was not her first rodeo. She's cheerleading at football games on fucking Saturday nights, not basketball games on Tuesdays.

Anthony took a few steps back. Dave and I waited for our gal to do the hang down and drop, but instead she leapt like a deranged lunatic. She flew fifteen feet and completely overshot our waiting arms. Calamity ensued, and there were legs and pea coats everywhere, as Alex landed in the capable but unsuspecting arms of

Anthony. Unfortunately, Anthony was *not* ready for the combination of Alex and fifteen feet of downward acceleration. Based on a slow-motion playback of the video, we can see that Anthony was absolutely crushed. He probably could have pressed charges. Alex, on the other hand, promptly stood up and walked off unharmed. We picked Anthony up and dusted him off, but he wobbled violently and crashed to the ground. Suddenly an (actual) Australian off-duty nurse came running over. *Den't git up, ya need to ring an ambo to the doc shop stat, love!* she shouted. Dave was so happy a *real* Australian had appeared that he just started screaming at our girls, *THAT'S HOW AN AUSTRALIAN SOUNDS. THAT'S HOW YOU SHOULD SOUND IF YOU'RE GOING TO DO AN AUSTRALIAN ACCENT THE ENTIRE FUCKING NIGHT!*

Two hours later, we found ourselves in some midtown hospital. Anthony was sharing a room with a really upbeat gunshot victim. He was such a good sport and was very talkative, relative to the number of bullets in his body. Anthony wasn't going anywhere for a while, so Dave, the girls, and I left him and his new buddy to get some rest.

Dave tried the bulldog-apartment line again and our cheerleaders obliged immediately. This seemed strange. Ordinarily, we would expect these girls to be running away from us as fast as possible. Then it hit me. These girls had nowhere to stay. They were gambling on this date more than we were! These girls were worried about securing the basics: they were after food and shelter and we were their providers. At some point on the walk home, I pulled Dave aside and explained my theory to him. We were responsible for these gals! We got them home safe and tucked them into Dave's bed and retired ourselves to the floor fort, where we woke up to some nice insect bites. The next morning, we bought them breakfast and went back to the hospital. Alex had ruptured Anthony's patellar tendon. One major surgery and eight months of recovery later, he was good as new.

The Purge

(Dave)

So much of where Mike and I come from is our old man. I like him a lot. I admire him very much. I respect the hell out of him. I don't want to be like him, though. No way. I want to have the good and righteous qualities he does, but I don't want to be *like* him. That would require me to change my entire personality, and I've been working on my personality for years.

We're different. John Stangle boasts a puritan work ethic, whereas I regularly introduce myself as "Snake" to parents I meet for the first time. My dad and I love each other. We always have. He is a great dad and a great man. He makes my mom happy, he fixes stuff, and he drinks Busch heavies. What's not to like? We haven't always liked each other, though. Some parents don't like their kids during the teenage years. Is this surprising to anyone? Teenagers are fucking shitheads. They think they know everything. I thought I knew everything. My dad actually *did* know everything, and he didn't like that I was sure I did, too, despite the fact that I was obviously a fucking idiot.

These days, we're a-okay. I'm twenty-nine now! I have a job, I'm no longer a financial burden on him, and I haven't gotten any chicks pregnant. (Just need to confirm this one—does the publisher provide fact checkers?) If my relationship with my dad were a credit score, I'd be in the 700s. I attribute a lot of that to his attitude shift once all the kids were out of college. If I had three male shithead kids and one female diva kid to put through grade school, high school, and college, I'd be a hard-ass, too! Tough luck, old man. You shouldn't have been humping Mom so much back in the eighties. You signed up for this.

Since we've all become young adults, he has mellowed in a noticeable way. Things that used to set him off now just escape his body through a shoulder shrug. His skin is thicker than leather. He is now a wise old sage, relaxed and comfortable in his life, and a great time to hang around with. Most people think of their "prime" as occurring somewhere in their twenties, physically speaking, or their thirties, forties, and fifties, professionally speaking. Papa Stangle waited to peak until after he knew his entire flock would make it into the real world alive and in at least decent condition. By 2008, the Stangle kids had shown enough promise for my father to take a breath, have a drink, and actually go at it with his wife for the first time since Bush #1 was in office. "Nineteen nineties Dad" was the absolute polar opposite of "Golden Age Dad." Nineteen nineties JT Hard-ass stood over us on Saturday afternoons as he took the role of Chore Czar while we scrubbed the *shit* out of our bathroom floors. Golden Age Dad hangs out in the hot tub he built (literally), a cigar in his mouth and chuckling at the off-color stories his kids tell him. Before, when going out at night, I'd regularly hear a solemn "Behave" as I would run past his chair with booze hidden in my back pocket. Nowadays, Golden Age Dad tells me to "wrap it up." Talk about progress! (Also, ew Dad. No!)

But before that progress? He didn't always like me.

Have you guys ever seen that horror movie called *The Purge*? Me neither. No way. No fucking way. I was too scared. I *hate* scary movies, and it's not because I'm a wimp. I *am* a wimp, but that's not why. Spiders scare me, just like they do anyone else. I'll admit that. Fuck spiders. Heights? You heard it here first. I'm six feet four and afraid of heights. But being wimpy isn't why I hate scary movies. It's because I'm a fucking human. Why would I see a scary movie and *choose* to be terrified for two hours of my life? Who volunteers for that? What is the matter with you all? Fuck that. Isn't watching a scary movie just the emotional version of cutting yourself? And you think *I'm* the sicko?

I do know what *The Purge* is about, though. The idea is pretty wild. In a futuristic society, once a year for twenty-four hours, any and all crime is legalized. There are no laws whatsoever. The premise is that human beings are evil and will commit crimes and do bad deeds, because it's inherently in their nature. The Purge is their opportunity to get it out of their systems. Three hundred sixty-four perfectly peaceful days are worth one bad day. I actually like the idea. I think I'd just take a bunch of fun hallucinogenic drugs and reenact that scene from the first Batman movie with Michael Keaton, where the Joker and his beret-wearing goons break in and gas the entire museum, blast a boom box over their shoulders with Prince playing, and spray-paint priceless artifacts. I could do that for Purge Day *Every. Fucking. Year.*

So why am I talking about *The Purge* so much? Because long before the movie came out, my old man and I were basically maintaining our shred of a functional family relationship by getting our deep-seated issues out of our systems in an annual father-son *Purge*-like battle. One fight a year, so the other 364 days would be peaceful.

SPOILER ALERT: Since starting this tradition I am 0-13. Zero wins, thirteen losses. We don't even need to do it anymore to get along; it's just that I can't go out without at least one victory. Every year that goes by, he gets older. He is sixty-two now! He is old as *shit*. I'm not retiring. Not now. He has plantar fasciitis, for Christ's sake! I'm due, God damn it.

Before you get all John Kreese[1] on me, laughing at my 0-13 record, you should know a little bit of background about my old man. John Thomas Stangle Jr. is the oldest of nine wild kids, a record-holding runner who could do a mile in under four minutes, who briefly played hoops

---

1   Shame on you if you don't know who John Kreese is. Uh, that bad guy from *Karate Kid*? I hope 90 percent of you just said "Oh yeah" and the other 10 percent of you just shut the fucking book. RIP, Mr. Miyagi, by the way.

at Syracuse, and who went on to be a three-time judo gold medalist in the Empire State Games. Again, that's judo (a hybrid of martial arts and dick-swinging swagger). He always used to quote his old sensei in this really unintentionally racist Oriental sort of accent, *"No much juuuudo, but you stwoooong rike bearcat!"*

That old man is tough as nails. He's had a mustache for as long as I've known him. He actually had a full-on lumberjack beard through his late twenties. But when our older brother, Sean, threw up all over it when he was little, JT did some damage control with a first-generation Philips Norelco and came out with the mustache.

Shall I go on? I once saw him put a camel in a headlock, because he considers spitting rude. It's rumored he was mistaken for Tupac a week before Tupac's death and got shot up while running errands. Not only did he not succumb to his wounds, he also kept it a secret so the real hit on Tupac would go off unspoiled, all because he doesn't approve of rap. Okay, those last two are a stretch, but here's a nugget of truth: he once bit a dog in the leg because the dog bit him first. It happened when he was twenty-seven and in line at McDonald's. Apparently there was a dog in McDonald's? He never explains that part. What he will explain is how the "little squirt" of a dog bit him in the ankle, so he responded by dropping to his knees, grabbing the dog's hind leg, and biting it like a caveman. What makes this story even better? The dog belonged to the lady he was working for at the time. I think she was actually buying him lunch, because he was building her an inground swimming pool. He didn't even get fired. The dog got put in time-out, and JT went back to her house and built the shit out of that pool. It's unknown if the dog survived the leg bite.

• • •

When you're 0-13, you have to look at your record differently than you would if you had squeezed out one or two wins. If I were 2-11, I could go into every year's fight trying to remember what I did right for those two victories. I'd have something to work from. There are no two victories. There isn't even one. I'm not on the board. Instead, I look at my *near* victories versus my most humiliating defeats. This strategy has allowed me to compile a highlight reel. There are a few Purges I can vividly remember, because:

1. I was not severely concussed afterward, and

2. For at least a slight moment during the bout, *I had a fucking chance to win.*

These were the deadliest Purges.

Purge III—Poolside Choke-Out.

I was in eighth grade for Purge III and really coming into my own shitheadedness. All my buddies were older guys. They were well past eighth grade, already causing a ruckus in high school, and I wanted a taste! I had access to new chicks, baggy jeans, Smash Mouth CDs, and a completely unjustified chip on my shoulder so big it cast a shadow over my head. My sister, Kristen, was already in high school. She was only a sophomore but dominated the Shaker High School swim scene, because she is basically part dolphin. JT loved watching her swim meets. I never understood the draw or why he made me watch every single one with him. Maybe he had a thing for one-pieces? But I was there, bored within minutes and looking for a distraction. Not him, though. He would sit and watch every swim meet from start to finish. Kudos, Dad. We're wired quite differently, you and I. Toward the end of Kristen's swim season, I was getting tired of sitting around doing nothing while all my buddies were running around doing something that was a combination of stupid, illegal, dangerous, and involving stolen lacrosse equipment. I had the itch. I was sniffing around for some excitement.

On the day of Purge III, JT and I were off to a bad start. He was pissed at me because he found three bags of empty Busch Light cans in our tree house in the yard and was unfairly pinning the blame squarely on me. His anger and my refusal to accept responsibility (coupled with my *horrible* poker face) were putting us at odds. What started at a whisper quickly escalated to a shouting match. And, after I ended one of my comebacks by addressing my dad as "pal," it became a full-on pushing match. Don't ever call your dad "pal" in an argument.

We were instantly wrestling outside my sister's high school swim meet. I don't remember much of it, because he choked me out right away. What a spectacle! We were two giant gladiators doing their worst to one another. An old-fashioned duel! Except most duels don't end with the loser waking up in the back of the winner's van as the winner is driving it home and laughing his ass off. He won by putting me in a sleeper hold. Do you know why they call it a sleeper hold? Because it puts you to fucking sleep. How did no one object to this? A dad chokes out his son, throws him over his shoulder, and walks out of a public high school in the middle of the afternoon . . . and no one says a thing? Times have certainly changed.

Purge III was the Purge that gave me my first gulp of false confidence. I must have thought I had a chance at some point, probably when my dad was catching his breath from laughing so hard, when I thought I had figured out what it would take to beat him. I was all skin and bones but no meat. I was a boy, not a man. I had the frame, I just needed to grow into it. Just needed to get a little bigger, a little faster, a little stronger. That theory would eventually be proved utterly false in *Purge VI— Can a Dog Have His Day?* But it was my strategy for the time. Looking back now, I can't recall how I ever believed in my body that much. While writing this very chapter, I took a break to crack my back over the stool at my desk, lost my balance, and fell backward directly onto my head. Yeah, Dave, this body will get you there.

Purge IV—The Mistake in the Lake

After several Purges it began to seem less important to strategize for victory and more important to strategize for how to avoid total humiliation. Every summer, my family went to the same cabin on Brant Lake up in the Adirondacks. We didn't own the place; it belonged to my mom's mentor when she was an up-and-coming court reporter in the 1970s. The environment nowadays is pretty relaxed, but when we were teenagers, it was just fucking wild. The only thing I can compare it to is the scene in *Who Framed Roger Rabbit* when Eddie Valiant pulls through the tunnel into Toon Town and everyone is going bonkers. My brothers and I all had our girlfriends there, we were sneaking booze at every opportunity possible, the entire camp always smelled like grass, despite all of us swearing we didn't even know what grass smelled like. It was mayhem, and I was the leader. Not old enough to drink with the older kids, too old to do stupid kids' activities. I was stuck in the middle and looking for TROUBLE. At the other end of this was JT. All he wanted to do was relax. It was the only vacation he took all year. I'm pretty sure he didn't even want us there, but to have us there *and* causing trouble *and* stealing his booze? Purge IV was on!

This time, it started before I even knew it. We were both standing about knee-deep in the lake water, probably ten feet offshore. It was hot as shit; otherwise he never goes in the water, which might be why he has only owned one pair of swim trunks in the past ten years. My dad was half in the bag. It had been over ninety degrees that day, so he was up to about eleven Busch heavies to counter the heat. It's a sound strategy. What he didn't know was that shithead Dave filled a 7 Up bottle with his gin when he wasn't looking and had quietly and painfully (fucking gin!?) been slurping it all afternoon. The property was big, but not big enough for the two of us. Soon we found each other in front of the lake and both attempted to have a civil conversation. A wisecrack turned into an exchange, an exchange turned into some Jerry Springer–style face yelling, and at the first smell of blood, the heat was on.

I was thirteen years old, about six feet one, and skinny as a rail. I had speed on him, but not much strength. I couldn't let him exploit how much stronger than me he was. My only hope for survival was to avoid being put into a sleeper hold. I was immediately put into a sleeper hold. Son of a bitch! It's downright pathetic how helpless someone is while in a sleeper hold. There is nothing you can do. My dad rotated my body toward the shore to make sure everyone who had been watching the fight was truly paying attention. Mike claims that he and my father met eyes, and in that exact moment, eleven-year-old Mike promised himself he would *never* partici-pate in a Purge. Dad held me there and did nothing for a minute, just to make sure that anyone building a sand castle, having a margarita, taking a nap, or reading a book was now watching him. Think Russell Crowe in

Gladiator, "Give the people what they want!" As soon as he had the camp's full attention, he slowly began walking backward into the lake, deeper and deeper, taking me with him each step of the way. I felt like a shark had swum into shallow waters, latched on to my leg, and was dragging me out to sea. He walked me backward until we could both barely touch the lake floor. I have no idea how he held on to me with such little footing. Why was I so much more buoyant than he was? Is his inexplicably rock-hard potbelly made of cement? Once he got me into deep waters, he told me to "take a big ol' breath, Davie boy" and immediately plunged my head underwater. I had about 0.3 seconds to gasp for any oxygen at all before my head was buried in the sand that was at my feet just seconds ago. I was struggling so much to avoid drowning that I didn't realize what he was doing until I came up out of the water choking and swinging. My swings connected with nothing but air.

When I wiped the water out of my eyes, my dad was already ten feet toward shore, calmly walking out of the water. My swim trunks were draped over his shoulder like a towel after a workout. I was ass-naked thirty feet from shore, choking up lake water and rubbing sand out of my eyes. My friends, family, and high school girlfriend were all watching. I can remember trying to decide if I should keep fighting or if I should look for a sign that the Purge was over. When my dad walked out of the water, he whipped my trunks off his shoulder and no-look threw them at my older brother, who was sitting on a lawn chair playing Game Boy. My dad walked five more feet onto the beach, grabbed my mom around the waist, kissed her, and said, "Time for happy hour?" He never even bothered to look back over his shoulder. Purge IV was over; 0-4.

Purge VIII—Can a Dog Have His Day?

At least once in his career, even the biggest of all losers has a shot. Even Willy Loman made a sale at some point, right? I can remember the specific Purge that I really believed I had a shot at winning. It was the middle of my career, and I couldn't have positioned myself better. I was coming up on my first summer after my freshman year at Butler University in Indianapolis. Months earlier, I had called my dad to tell him that playing Division One lacrosse really stunk, and I didn't want to do it anymore. Did I mention that my place on that lacrosse team was arguably the *only* thing that pleased my dad during our thirteen-year "friction period"? He had all the gear, the mugs, the sweatshirts, the magnets. He traveled unlimited miles to watch me play, scrimmage, practice, anything. I could have been beating off in a public restroom, but if I had on lacrosse gear and did it with a mix of athletic style and aggression, he'd cheer me on. The only problem was that existence at Butler University was zero percent fun. Our freshman lacrosse class's average GPA our first semester (sixteen kids) was a 1.82. A 1-point-fucking-82! And that was the average, meaning some of us were *under* that! We were a pretty stressed group. As a side note, eleven of those sixteen eventually transferred out to other schools. I was just an eighteen-year-old kid with an appetite for fun, God damn it. We established a resistance. Every Thursday, Friday, and most Saturdays, we would buy a Weekender (a thirty-pack; credit: Mousey Lynch, RIP), sit three across in the Ross Hall men's bathroom with our pants around our ankles, and drink. You're reading this correctly. We had to act like we were taking a shit in order to sneak booze. Bottom line: Butler was miserable and getting worse. It was time to call home and break the news that I needed to transfer. My dad's disappointment was a real kick to the dick that I didn't need.

The one nice thing was I did come home from Butler with the body of a Greek fucking god. It was miserable to have to get up at 5 a.m. and sprint every morning. It was miserable to have to lift weights twice a day six days a week. It was miserable to drink never and exercise always. In general, being healthy is downright miserable. I guess it wasn't *that* miserable to be in incredible shape, though. I had the *body* of Michael Phelps but the bravado of Ryan Lochte. It was a deadly combination, and I couldn't wait for that year's Purge. If I ever stood a chance, this was it. By the end of my second semester, I had made a nice rebound with my grades and thought that might have started off my summer in the right place with JT. A "nice rebound" was a relative term, as JT would point out, because it would have been *tough for*

me to fall off the floor. Good point, JT. Doesn't mean we
can't get along this summer, right? Oh, Dad, did I mention I'm miserable at Butler and I'm not going back?
Where am I going? To the State University of New York at
Geneseo—the college no one has heard of, unless you're
a teacher or a farmer, or both. Why am I transferring
there? Because the gal to guy ratio is 6:1 and all people
do there is rage. *That's* why I'm going.

I could see why he wasn't happy with my life choice.
That I concealed my true, degenerate interior with a
lacrosse-playing persona was just about the only thing
my dad liked about me at the time. It was no wonder
we fought within literally *minutes* of me arriving home
from Indiana that summer. The night before, I was fourteen hours into the seventeen-hour drive and decided
to stop at a friend's school for the night, before hitting
the homestretch the next day. For a few *very* silly legal
reasons that are somehow still an issue ten years later,
I won't get into just how I got arrested at my buddy's
school that night. But I will tell you that it involved
Senators Club whiskey, and an *alleged* "all-you-can-eat"
buffet at Ponderosa. That next day, somehow, someway,
news of my arrest traveled back to Menands faster than
I did. To this day, I don't know how he knew, but when
I pulled into the driveway that next morning, JT was
standing on the front lawn, hands on the hips of his
cargo shorts. I was so fucked. I started heavy breathing.
I got nervous. I felt like Luke Skywalker running around
that swamp with Yoda's balls on the back of his neck:

Remember your training! I was jacked up—psychologi-
cally, yes, but also physically. This was my day!

I got out of the car and immediately started yelling.
I don't know what I was even yelling about. I just knew
that if I yelled loud enough, I wouldn't hear the things
my father was yelling simultaneously. He apparently
had the same exact strategy. We were standing face-to-
face, screaming total nonsense. At one point, I think I
might have even kicked dirt on his shoes. It didn't take
long for us to come to blows. No matter how strong I
was then, how much I thought I was his physical match,
I learned very quickly that with the sole exception of
retard strength, nothing compares to old-man strength.
He had me pinned within seconds. I think he'd still have
me there with my face smushed into the grass on my
front lawn had Denise not come outside screaming for it
to end. It was over before it started, Mom.

I've battled my father over thirteen grueling Purges,
through my entire adolescence, and lost every fucking
time. When JT and I started our annual battle, I was
fourteen. I was young and dumb, and (soon to be) full of
cum. I thought I knew the way! When I finally got my shit
together and retired? I was in my mid-twenties. It took
me until then to realize that *maybe JT was onto something all along.* Maybe I was the shithead.

The Hunt

Let's Be Offensively Honest

A Little Something for the Ladies

*A Look into a Man's Psyche,
at the Expense of Your Respect*

(Mike)

We have very few single female friends who *want* to be single. Some do; maybe they want to focus on their careers or they're just trying to shake a tough case of the broken-heart blues. If you're one of those gals, skip this chapter. But by and large, most single gals don't want to be single. "Single Ladies" isn't just one of Dave's top five songs of all time; it represents a large population of modern-day gals who share one common circumstance: they've got no man. Everyone has female friends who desperately want boyfriends. It happens to most females at some point in the five years following college. Or always. The reasons don't matter much. Maybe you're feeling the pressure from your folks, because they were married by twenty-two. Maybe you've got some insecurities about growing old alone. Maybe it's because all your friends are doing it. Hey, maybe you just need the D *all the time*. Maybe it's science.

We get it. Game on. It's hunting season. We know you gals in cities like New York and D.C. have it rough. The competition is nuts! City gals are hot! And there are tons of them. They're everywhere. Even if they aren't, it doesn't make it any easier. All you San Fran gals don't know what to think, because the fellas there are mostly into other fellas. Whether you're in the burbs or a city, we get how tough your competition is. We also get how picky that allows us guys to be. I've been getting girls that are light-years out of my league for . . . light-years! *Plus,* on top of that, most of us are total dickheads. Mike sure is. I've seen that kid blow off dates because he ate too many Gushers, and he is twenty-five years old! It's hard out there, and we get that. We're not defending guys; we're trying to help you deal with these idiots so you can eventually be stuck with one. Make sense? Nope, not for us, either.

Do you ever look at certain guys and wonder why they are more successful with women? More than likely, they've learned what women want and they play into that. You should do the same thing with guys. Dave owns like sixty pairs of shoes. He has *seasonal shoes*! Do most guys do that? No. Do you think he has so many shoes because he *loves* shoes? Nope. But you love shoes, and it's the first thing you look at when you meet him. Oh look at that, he's off to a good start with you. Good for you, Dave. She's cute.

Let's get on with a look inside our heads. We hope this helps with the fellas, you man-hunters. You can hate us for now, but we expect an invite to the wedding.

1. Where are the best hunting grounds? Uh, we don't fucking know.

Where are you going tonight? Go to a bar. Don't go to a club. No one meets his or her husband at a club unless you're Pitbull or Pitbull's wife (lucky gal). That hot guy you spotted last week at a club with a name from a Stefon sketch . . . he might have been spending enough money for you to rationalize away any concerns over his multiple tribal tattoos, but he's wearing a reflective shirt with an eagle on it. Is he the future Mr. You? Again, not unless you're the future Mrs. Bull. Skip the club, go to a bar. There are always guys there, and we'll be drinking, so we won't be such pussies. Another disclaimer: we're not saying a bar is the best place to meet guys, it's just the place we're most likely to be, and we really want to meet you.

Next, science. Use it to your advantage. Remember the big picture: Men like sex. It motivates us. It drives us. There are other things in life that are important to us, of course, but we forget what they are. Sex, as an underlying theme to everything in our lives, is literally built into our DNA. If you meet a guy who you don't think took a brief second in his brain to consider what it would be like to have sex with you prior to engaging in *any* conversation with you, you're wrong. We're so good at it, our brains are capable of giving any girl a complete sexual pat-down in less than two seconds, while simultaneously asking about her grandmother's health. If you can't pick up on that, it only means he's doing a really great job of hiding it. Or he's gay (so jealous). Or he *just* got laid right before meeting you, so getting laid again isn't his top physiological priority for several minutes. Still, even at that point, he is thinking, *Wait, but there's the future to think about.* . . . You think that makes us pigs? Probably. But sadly, your opinion of us doesn't change your luck or put you any closer to your goals. It only crosses two more guys off your list, so your odds with the male population just went down slightly. What is your other option? Embrace it, play into it. Use it to your advantage. Our gals The Betches figured this out early, and they win at everything. Oh, these brothers read the Betches? Okay, now you're thinking that maybe you should hear us out. Let's go back inside the bar and talk, okay? We didn't bring up the sex-is-in-our-DNA caveman reality so that you'll think we're telling you to sleep with bar guys right away. Just go into that bar understanding that's going to be *our* plan. *We* are thinking about sleeping with you right away. Please accept this as more honest than disgusting. Remember the sexual pat-down guys do. If he's talking to you, that means he's already had these sexual thoughts about you, and he liked them! You're past Step 1.

2. Oh Sweet Mother of God, Dress the Part, Would You?

Deciding what kind of arrows to put in your quiver? Don't listen to your girlfriends. Just don't. They are in the same boat you are. If they are giving out advice, it's only based on their own failures at this very process you're trying to conquer. It's the blind leading the blind! In fact, that is Rule #1: Don't take guy advice from a girl who is frustrated with guys. Your girlfriends who are most likely to preach to you about guys are probably pigs named Samantha who are terrible with guys. Stop listening to Samantha's bitter advice, which she doles out while swiping right on Tinder with reckless abandon. Instead, listen to your inner guy. Start thinking like a guy. How do we guys think? Start with the basics. How will you come off in our sexual pat-down?

What are you wearing, anyway? Don't wear a shirt with ruffles or different cool sleeves that other girls think is sexy because it's classy. It isn't. In fact, fuck sleeves. Show some arm, girl! Show some everything. We're guys, we love skin. Guys like butts and boobs. One, the other, both. That's it. Until things progress for us beyond conversations, drinks, jokes, and getting to know each other, there are really only two things: boobs and butts. Four things, if you count them all separate, butt cheeks and all. Wear jeans. If you don't look good in jeans, wear a skirt. Skirts are awesome; show some leg. Tank tops? We love tank tops. If the material of whatever you are wearing is tight around your chest, we like that. You already know that! There are boobs under there. If your goal is to attract a guy, and you *know* that guys like boobs, and you *have* boobs—what kind of fucked-up logic tells you to do the opposite of "flaunt them"? Are you afraid other girls will judge you for this? The ones wearing tight shirts won't; they're too distracted by all the attention they're getting from guys.

If you do wear something on the tighter or more revealing side, we'll probably sneak a few looks at those boobies. Don't be offended by this. Dogs aren't offended when another dog sniffs their butt. You *can* be offended if we sniff your butts (before the third date), but let the boob stare go. We try to discreetly hide these sneaks. We're just curious! Remember, you can find it offensive, or translate it through your new think-like-a-guy strategy and take it as a compliment, a positive sign of interest. Do you know what our ideal social setting is? It's one where we're wearing sunglasses that hide our eyes, where everyone is drunk, and every girl is in a bikini. So yes, basically a beach. Now you *know* that. Do you think Mike has insisted on living in Nantucket for the last four summers because he loves the architecture? The beach is a lifeline to our dicks! This gets me thinking, why would he live on the beach for this long and *not* get in sick shape? Half-assing it, if you ask me. I visit him every summer and am on a strict diet of air and cigarettes the entire month before I get there. I treat it like ladies treat their weddings. I'm on diuretics on even days and pulling the trigger after dinners on odd days. The beach is a man's sexual Graceland! No guy expects "the beach" setting to be the norm, but think about why it appeals to us and work from there. Revealing clothes, hidden eyes, booze, happy vibe. Why not appeal to that? We don't expect you to come to a bar in a bikini; just remember what drives us when you're putting your outfit together.

3. Don't Say Shit That Every Girl Says

Remember that viral fad of videos popping up titled "Shit ___ Girls Say?" Shit Jewish Girls Say, Shit New York Girls Say, Shit Single Girls Say, Shit Black Girls Say. Do you realize that you and your friends inspired this entire Shit Girls Say movement? It's only funny because it's true. We've all heard it all. I'm sure you have, too, but hey, I'M TALKING HERE.

When you meet a guy, don't tell him about your gluten allergy. If you have cats, maybe wait to reveal that. If you're super-religious, that's cool. Just file that away with the cats and bring it up once the bond gets a little stronger. Don't talk about how close your family is. Everyone is close with their family, or at least wants to be. If not, and you have daddy issues, Dave requests that you give him a call. Wheelhouse! Family is important, sure, but not yet. We'll get to that way down the line. You've got to concentrate on keeping our attention; it gets lost very easily. Get back to what motivates men: sex. We're not saying you should start talking dirty right out of the gate, unless you want to. You could see how that goes if you'd like; we'll be at Whiskey Town tonight. We're just saying to err on the side of flirtatiousness. That seems obvious, but you'd be surprised how warped your energy can get.

Don't ask what we do within three questions. We know that is a big one for you, but hide it like we're hiding our desire to grab your ass. We don't make one of our first three questions "What would it be like to be inside you?" That's what the sexual pat-down is about. If you want to know what we do (read: how much money we make) just look at our clothes, our shoes, check for ear piercings, then make an unfair but somewhat educated guess. In fact, the next time a gal asks what one of us does within three questions, we're just going to start grabbing butts. Then all our cards will be on the table.

Smile a lot! We're more insecure than you think. You like us when we're confident, so if you want us to be confident, then remind us that it's going well. When you break it down, we're actually pretty simple: If we're talking to you, we're interested. If we're not, we're not.

4. Okay, Now What? Get Him Hooked. Maybe Give Him a Hand Job. With Your Vagina.

Mike and I differ on this. Mike believes that in most cases, if you want it to go somewhere, you shouldn't sleep with him right away. That's not totally accurate; he thinks BJs are a nice treat after a first date. He just doesn't want to pressure the gal, okay? He loves treats; such a dog. I'm a firm believer that you should sleep with him right away, even if it isn't going anywhere. Worst case: you both get off, and then go back to the drawing board less sexually frustrated. Okay, I suppose that isn't the *worst case* that comes from sleeping around, but my message is that it's 2015. As long as you're safe, have yourself some fun. Whether it goes somewhere great or nowhere at all, if you can involve sex, why the hell not? It's either no strings attached or the exact strings you're looking for! That could just be the twenty-nine-year-old in me talking.

The best approach probably lies somewhere right in the middle of how Mike and I look at it. Leaving something to be desired does drive us guys crazy; it keeps our attention, and it gets you in our heads. Sleeping with us shows us what you've got, and vice versa. If you're getting calls from us afterward, it means we really liked it. We want more. If not, then maybe Mike had a point. Either way, the sex part is going to be bigger than you'd like to admit in the infancy of a fostering relationship. We know it sounds shallow, but these are the facts! Kind of.

Want to know what a guy likes in the sack? You should probably check out some porn. Mike can refer you to several free websites if you'd like. Even if you don't like porn, you should watch some. And drop the degrading-to-women act, Janeane Garofalo. Anyone see that movie *Don Jon* with Joseph Gordon-Levitt? JGL is the man. He breaks down porn as a man's guilty pleasure versus romantic comedies as a lady's guilty pleasure. It appeals to our nature, just like the sappy shit appeals to yours. Fellas who are good at being sweet have seen their share of romantic comedies; gals who are dynamite in the sack have seen their share of porn. Sure, some porn is degrading to women. I won't go on the record as being against much, but that weird porn just freaks me out. When I was in college and online porn was just coming of age, we used to check out this site called cockgaggers.com. Don't look it up, it's not there anymore. Weirdly, I think that means cockgaggers got bought out by a bigger operation? I've got to think it was for the name and not the content, which was pretty literal to the name. It was just women on their knees with guys fucking their mouths like jackhammers. It was awful. Scarring.

Sometimes they would put a toilet seat over the girl's head, then do it. Now *that's* degrading! I'm not going to say I didn't laugh a few times; the sounds were just so ridiculous! Still, cockgaggers didn't exist for college kids to laugh at, not exclusively, anyway. There were guys out there who were going to cockgaggers because it fit their preferences. You think *we're* sick pups? Those guys are the real sick pups. Most porn isn't like that, though. Most porn that the general population of men likes consists of a movie in which a man is directing one or more women to do things based on what turns the viewers on. The viewers are all men! Do you think the first girl to look up at a guy while giving him a blow Johnson just thought it up herself? *You know, I'm tired of looking at this guy's belly button. I think I'll multitask and give head while en-gaging in a staring contest.* No way! A guy asked the girl to do it, because it turns guys on! Connect the dots.

Whether you like porn or not, there is no arguing that the pornographic community can teach you tons of tricks that will drive men absolutely wild. Are we suggesting the first time you get under the sheets with a fella you throw his legs over his head and start licking his butt hole? Maybe. No, but don't forget how addictive good sex can be. Sex is a drug, an addictive drug. The only side effect is you *might* end up in an incredibly destructive two-year relationship in which no party can walk away, because each is deeply addicted to having sex with the other. Just ask Dave about Big Sex sometime. That, my friends, is what we call a good problem to have. It's pretty rare, though; we're simply talking here about sex with people you're courting. Why let it be boring? Why refrain from standing out when you clearly have the ability? I've had relationships with women that were built *purely* on sex. I've had girlfriends, legit girlfriends, whom I was so into solely because the sex was worth whatever else I had to put up with. You have this power, ladies. You're in our *brains*. What are you going to leave imprinted there? Let your freak flag fly a little bit.

Sex is changing. You need to keep up or you'll fall behind. Just doing the stuff you grew up doing isn't going to cut it anymore. Keep up with the trends. Change things up. You aren't still wearing jelly sandals, are you? No! You're walking around in a hot pair of Tory Burch wedges fucking shit up left and right. It works the same way with sex. We're not talking about lingerie. Little secret: girls love lingerie and think guys do, but we don't really care. We care in the sense that we're about to have some really enthusiastic sex, but you can skip the lacey shit. It's cool to get into, but think of it like wrapping paper—do people like wrapping paper because it's nice or because it encourages them to rip it to shreds to get to what's underneath? You know the drill, so know the trends. What used to be considered sexy is boring. What used to be considered taboo is now sexy. The blowjob is a fine example. BJs have been around for a while, but weren't a regular thing until the 1960s and '70s. We can't verify that, but Mike did just look it up. He googled "when did blowjobs get so popular?" We plan on reading the array of results later on tonight, as well as the sponsored ads, but we'll just stick with the seventies for now, because that looks to be the general consensus. Regardless of if they became big in the seventies, were perfected in the eighties, or just got weird in the nineties, the fact remains that giving head grew in popularity for three very connected reasons, listed in ascending order of importance: 1) Head is awesome. 2) Men love head. 3) Girls started giving it regularly. Don't you think in the seventies, when blowjobs were a new thing, there were a group of women who refused, because it seemed indecent? Of course there were. *Don't be those girls!* They probably had to move to Canada to marry draft dodgers, while all the red-blooded American blowjob enthusiasts were taking home soldiers with a dozen confirmed kills each. We'd just like to take this opportunity to point out that we *know* you like getting head, too. And luckily, we usually like going down on you! We know a lot of times it's a trust and comfort thing with you gals, and we get that. But seriously . . . if we go down on you, it tells you a few things.

1. We think you're clean. We're not going to get all up into somethin' if we don't think you're hygienically sound.

2. We want you to get off! We want to turn you on! We are interested in you outside of our own selfish sexual needs.

Moving on. You know what the next "blowjob" of our generation is? Nudie shots. Like it or not, these things are here to STAY. In fact, they are only evolving, and if you haven't jumped on board now, you'd better download Snapchat before it's too late. Yes, we realize how absurd this reality may seem. Yes, we realize that they can get you in trouble. And yes, we fucking love them. That doesn't mean you can't be smart about it. Not everyone needs to be Paris Hilton or Kim Kardashian, though you should take a minute to think about where they would be *without* those sex tapes. Be smart about them. In fact, being smart about it makes it even hotter. Whoever the girl was who invented the nudie-shot pose where you hold a cell phone in front of your face and snap a picture, flash on, in front of a mirror . . . she deserves a medal. She started it all. She gave the first Class of 2006 "blowjob." I'll tell you another thing: she isn't single. She drove some guy nuts with those pictures and is sitting on the front porch of the mansion he bought her, sipping a nice sweet tea. You can, too. Some girls don't send them, because they don't believe their bodies are sexy. This is the worst mistake you can make. If you know a man is attracted to you, make him think that you *know* you are sexy.

Quit judging other chicks, too. It's a competitive world out there. I know guys who do the cheesiest stuff to get laid. They do stuff I'd never do, but there's still no comeback to someone looking at you and pointing at the scoreboard. Consider this: Most guys like me. They just do. I'm typically pretty popular around my fellow man. My personality allows me to hang in the upper echelon of male friendships. I'm often invited to popular social events. I'm nice, never have problems with fellow fellas, and I'm not that exclusive. Asian people find me hilarious, black people find me goofy, German people often say, "You're kinda what we were going for, back then." As far as I know (or think), when guys think of me, they generally don't say, "Fuck that guy."

What if I was a girl, though? What if I had the same exact personality, same exact lifestyle, but I was a gal? I'd still be a cute brunette, I'll tell ya that much. Don't worry about that. What I *would* be worried about is how other gals thought of me. Every other gal would have a major, major problem with me. I do so many things in my everyday life as a guy that gals just plain hate about other gals. I'd have no friends. I'd be included in nothing. You know when you hear a bunch of gals just trashing some slut? I'd be that slut. I'd be sleeping around *so* much. I can barely control my sex drive as is; my only blessing is that it's super-hard to get laid when you're a giant dufus. Imagine if I were a gal, and the only thing I needed to do to get laid was be slutty? Dave as a gal equals game over. I'd be showing off my tits way too much. I would own several high-waisted bikini bottoms. I would shave intricate and creative shapes and patterns into my pubic hair. I bet some jock that I sleep with would tell the entire school after he banged me, then whatever theme I had going above my slow cooker (that's what I'd call my vagina if I were a gal) would somehow become incorporated into my high school nickname. Later on in life, I would become the chick who causes wives to elbow their head-cocked husbands in the ribs when they check me out as I roller-skate by on the boardwalk. Heyyy (wink). Nailed it!

Whoa, how did we get this lost? Still, key takeaways: boobs and butts, don't be "that girl," and for Pete's sake, don't shoot the messenger! Unless you're shooting us a nudie pic.

Breaking Up

Man, This Stinks

(Dave)

Mike and I are not the face of single men in America. We might be soon, after publication of this book, since we're both currently single and no woman will ever speak to us again. That doesn't change the past, though; we've both had girlfriends aplenty. We've had long-term and short-term girlfriends. We've had some fun-while-it-lasted girlfriends and some I-must-have-been-on-dirty-Sprite girlfriends. Me specifically? I've had a few really intense long-term girlfriends. I had one in high school, a total babe named Nikki. We lost our virginity to each other when we were fifteen years old. It was classic high school sex, too. House party, keg of beer, full bush, not a rubber within ten square miles. Those were the days. She was a super-religious gal and came from a really devout family. I remember her mother wouldn't let her younger sister (who I imagine also grew up to be a babe) read Harry Potter books, because they were "blasphemy." Nikki eventually dumped me for the guy she would end up marrying, I think. Maybe there was one guy in between us. Facebook didn't exist then, so I couldn't properly stalk her. Whoever it was, it didn't matter, I was so sad. It was the first time I got dumped, my first overall breakup.

Don't feel bad for me, I deserved to get dumped. I cheated on her all the time. It was high school! Everyone was following their dicks! I deserved to get dumped a thousand times over. That doesn't mean I wasn't devastated. It was actually worse, because I got dumped *and* I deserved it. I don't think I truly got over it until she emailed me years later to let me know she was engaged to be wed and that she told the guy she was engaged to that *he* was her first and only. Whaaaaaaaat? Up until that point, she was always lingering in the back of my head, fucking around and causing a psychological ruckus. When she told me she was a born-again virgin, it was like ripping off the Band-Aid. I just didn't care anymore. Somewhere out there, for the rest of Nikki's life, Dave Stangle would be her little secret. I felt so bad for her husband that I started to feel better about myself. Boom, over it! I would be hesitant to write all this down and blow her cover, but if Harry Potter is blasphemy, then what is this book? Pure. Evil. I'm in the clear. They won't even sell this book at the Christian stores she shops at, anyway.

I had a pretty serious girlfriend in college, too. Nancy! Sweet, sweet Nancy. Nancy was probably my favorite out of all the girlfriends I've had. We're still very good friends to this day, sweet Nancy and I. We were a great match and had a fantastic relationship. In the end, the timing just wasn't right. I was a young whippersnapper fresh out of college; she was light-years ahead of me on the maturity scale. She wanted to get more out of her weekends than heading to the East Village and blacking out at Whiskey Town every Saturday. And Thursday. And Friday. And some Wednesdays, if the weather was nice. When that breakup happened, it was just no fun at all. I was losing someone who I knew was a great fit, but I also knew it wasn't going to work without one of us sacrificing our priorities before we were ready.

I went on a real tear of ugly chicks after her. I was knocking them down like bowling pins. That's the high-est compliment you can pay an ex-girlfriend, it means you're taking the breakup really hard. During those dark days, I realized and started living out a theory that would consume my mid-twenties. If I only made love to women with great bodies and ugly faces, or vice versa, I'd never want to date them seriously! Shallow? Yes. But this selec-tion process was incredibly effective in staving off fruit-less relationships after a hard breakup. I was taking it hard. So was every six in midtown Manhattan. Ayo!

The last true breakup I ever had really turned my life upside down. It was my first adult breakup; you know, when things matter. It also taught me all I need to know about breakups for the rest of my life. That is, I never want to fucking do it again. My last girlfriend was Big Sex. Big Sex was a real wild card. She was very funny and quirky, pretty crazy, and in hindsight an absolutely terrible match for me. It's understandable how I missed that last part, though, once you put your eyes on her. She was tall, slender, blond (classic Dave!), and was really, really good-looking. My dad had a legit crush on her. He got all bashful when she came around and he would make these attempts to flirt with her that were so transparent it was kind of adorable. I'd always squeeze her big ol' butt in front of him, too, just to get him jealous. It was like he was mad at me for dating her, as if I was somehow getting away with something. She had these incredible boobs that I was *convinced* were fake the first several times I came on them. She was something. She was crazy, but my kind of crazy. I like the crazy ones. Can't help it, always have and always will.

For a time, Big Sex just worked for me. She was a smart, driven, successful girl with a nice family. Her craziness was buried deep, deep down inside of her, and for one reason or another, I just found and released it. It was like her body was one of those eighth-grade science fair volcanoes and somehow my penis was made of baking soda. Tupac said it: deadly combinations. It was a deadly combination that worked—for a while, anyway. She was always as drunk as me, always more out of control, always doing something over-the-top. It took me a very, very long time to come to the realization that our entire relationship was built on sex. When I think of her now, the only pleasant thought I have is that she was attractive in ways I had never known before. It was like she was wired specifically for me, like Lisa in *Weird Science*.

A relationship built purely on sex can only last so long. People say that as though it means it will 100 percent be short. They don't mention that it's a sliding scale. The more solid a sexual foundation it's built on, the longer it lasts. I dated Big Sex for two years before things started to chip away. Drama followed us everywhere. Maybe I was tit-blind, maybe I was in denial. At the height of our relationship, I would be late to work and early to home, all on the account of getting naked. We used to meet at my old midtown apartment at lunch for sandwiches and coitus. Do you know how great your afternoons are, coming off a turkey BLT and a mutually timed 'gasm that makes your neighbor's Pomeranian bark hysterically? BS and I were addicted to one another. Sex can be like a drug. It can take over your priorities, your motivations. It can turn you into a junkie. We were junkies. We were backroom, crack-house, belt-around-the-arm sex junkies. I can't wait for her spiteful rebuttal column to come out in *Redbook* after this book's publication. It'll be all like "Uh it wasn't that great." Hey, it was for *me*!

Eventually Big Sex and I got ourselves a nice apartment in a nice little neighborhood and had some big sex in it. A year later, it came time to renew our lease. Things were a little rocky with BS at the time. I was feeling a lot of pressure to grow up, put a ring on it, take the next step. I wasn't remotely ready for any of that shit, especially with someone so emotionally turbulent. I was committed to her, though. I thought re-upping our lease for another year might show her that. Nope. Did I mention we had a dog? Frank the Bulldog! Raising a bulldog with someone else is one off from having a full-blown human child.

BS dumped me the day before our new lease started. This was the last time I got dumped and the first time I perfected just how to come out of it. I couldn't do the depression thing again; I couldn't do "back to the drawing board." This chapter isn't about the drawing board. It's about handling a breakup like a fucking boss. It's about moving on, like the true sicko you are. You wondering why Mike hasn't chimed in yet? This little factoid might explain it. Consider Mike and me about even on the number of girlfriends scale. Serious, short-lived, long distance, whatever. For every Nikki, Sweet Nancy, and Big Sex, Mike has a roster of his own. What makes me the "expert" over Mike is that every single girlfriend I've ever had has dumped me. I've never been the dumper. I always get dumped! I have a 100 percent dump rate. Isn't that fucked up? *Now* you can feel bad for me.

How do you break the news to your buddies? What about your parents? Where do you sleep in the short term? How do you fill this new void in your life? Your penis: where do you put it?

After getting dumped more times than I can count, I'd like to think I know a little something-something about navigating my way through the Hurricane Sandy of emotions coming your way, flooding your shore house, and getting Chris Christie in your face with a megaphone. Here's my play, take it or leave it.

Step 1: Issue a Press Release

The world has to know. Address the rumors. Set the story straight. Don't be embarrassed; don't hide it, own it. If you're timid about it, you'll come off as weak. Even if there is a chance you and your ex might eventually get back together—it isn't now, otherwise you wouldn't have gotten dumped in the first place. If he/she dumps you just to get you to react, don't take them back. People who resort to that can't properly communicate and are also douche bags. You're single now. Own it. Your friends will all react, one way or another. Women want their friends to feel sorry for them when they get dumped. The best feeling a man can get is his friends being *excited* for him. When Big Sex gave me the boot back in the day, the rumors didn't take long to start swirling. We were living together at the time, so this was juicy to the outside world. I'm not a huge fan of always resorting to a sports analogy, but the following email got everyone on the same page pretty quickly:

Dave Stangle (dave.stangle@xxxxxx.com)
5/4/12
My Friends,

It has come to my attention that I should address some of the off the field issues concerning my playing career as well as my rumored free agency.

I have been with the Big Club for 2+ years now, some would say through the twilight of my career. I came up as a rookie in 2010 with nothing but my boyish charm and grim determination to win. Already considered a solid clubhouse presence, my first game back-to-back inside the park home runs made a splash with the Big Club immediately. I was on her radar rather quickly, and the rest was history. Since those days, I've built a home in the ballpark, taken on a budding protégé in AAA bulldog phenom Frankenstein, and run out every ground ball—no matter how silly or pedantic.

Sadly, after sitting with upper management and discussing my current contract at length, the Big Club has decided to let me go and to move in a different direction. Perhaps she is looking for a younger, more professional hitter . . . someone who concentrates on their raw footwork rather than making a web gem. Perhaps my lack of plate discipline or high strikeout rates on Saturday nights was too much to bear. Maybe having a little too much pine tar on my bat at times rubbed management the wrong way . . . but I'm a ballplayer, God damn it, and I was born this way. No matter what the issues were, I'll look back on my time with the Big Club with fond memories. I am glad there is no bad blood, and I even look forward to revisiting the clubhouse in the future (probably in August, when she misses me after a bad date and offers me a one-time, one-night appearance for Dave Stangle Bobble Head night).

That being said, I am looking forward to my free agency period—projected to last through at least 2016. I plan on taking my training seriously and visiting every ball club in the majors, multiple times. I'll take it all in. Spring Training . . . the Arizona Fall League . . . Dominican Winter League . . . AAA clubs in Murray Hill . . . hell, AA clubs! Don't be surprised if you catch me down at NYU poaching in High Single A ball either. There is some real talent down there.

I also plan on working with the game's best scouts. I am going to spend countless hours in the batting cage with Howard Freedman, one of the best hitting coaches in the game (as well as Ted Clifton, arguably the best bunter in the game). I'll be doing the bulk of my training at The Safe House at 41 St. Marks Place—5th floor. I'm confident that within The Safe House I'll find all the necessary elements for a ballplayer to succeed. My strength and conditioning coach, Anthony Hubbert, has promised to whip me into shape mentally, physically, and chemically. With hard work and determination, I will emerge as a 2016/2017 prize acquisition.

I look forward to meeting you in competition on the field!

Step 2: Okay, Now Get Out There and Get Weird

I've got a buddy named Tim. Today he is a ruthless titan of industry, a reckless socialite, and owns several custom-tailored pairs of pajama pants. Back when we all moved to New York City, though? Tim was an animal. He was the first person I ever heard say "Let's get weird!" with regularity, before everyone else started saying it. He would say "Let's get weird!" so often at Whiskey Town that the bar eventually had it printed on the back of their shirts. One could argue that was the original source of the entire phrase. Do you know how big that is? It's like starting the Macarena craze back in the nineties. No wonder Tim made it big. The writing was on the wall from day one. He had a point back then, too. Get weird. Hey, why the fuck not? No one is judging you.

Post-breakup is the biggest judgment-free zone one is ever allowed. No one will look twice. And if they do, it's because they *aren't* having enough fun in your newfound singleness. Mix it up. Don't say no. Sleep on a stranger's floor. Sleep on couches. Wake up across the border. Watch the sun come up. Black out before it goes down. If you're looking for inspiration, watch Mike for a night (fucking lunatic). You've got a perfectly legitimate excuse to act a fool. You've got nothing to lose. I'm not endorsing completely reckless behavior, but don't be shy. You have no commitments, no expectations, no limits. Hey, here's something you can do now that you couldn't do before—have sex with some different people. Actually, be reckless! Look at you, you're a catch! This is one of the few times in your life you can mow down everything in your path and all you'll ever hear is "good for you" followed by a firm pat on the back. The world is your oyster and that oyster has a vagina. Or a peener. Or maybe both! You need to get back out there. You need to make mistakes. You need to make a lot of mistakes. You need to sleep with people you don't actually feel anything for.

The accepted philosophy for so long has been that it's shameful to have sex with someone you don't care about. What about how nerve-racking it is to have sex with someone you *do* care about? You have to show up, be fair, bring your A-game, all your cards are already on the table. You already know your borders and hers, the stuff she will and won't do. And guess what? There are no surprises! Fuck that, I love surprises! Not *"Surprise! I have herpes!"* surprises, but cool and interesting ones where you think things like *Is she a squirter?* or, *How did she just make me pee a little?* One of the first completely random women I tricked into going to bed with me post-BS was this super-cute black chick. Yup! I had never been with a black chick before. When she took off her shirt and I had these awesome black chick boobies in front of me, I didn't even know where to start. I love boobs, and this was like having two *really* different and dark ones with Hershey's Kisses on them. The Hershey's Kisses were her nipples. Did you put that together? Oh, and as an added bonus, she looked like Hilary from *Fresh Prince*. Do you know how many times I beat off to Hilary as a kid? This was like beating off to Hilary . . . while *inside* Hilary! Total mind blower.

Don't be afraid to mix it up in a weird way, too. Lord knows I did. As long as you walk away clean and with a good story, then you'll be left in a better place than you were before. I once got mixed up with an older gal up in Saratoga Lake. I'm not even sure she qualified as a gal anymore; she was forty-five years old. Was she hot? Nope. Not remotely. Maybe in 1988, but probably not since 1995. She was a heavy smoker, pretty skanky. It doesn't take much to hook a guy so soon after a breakup, and it didn't take much to hook me. I'll never forget how just-attractive-enough for me she looked in her "JUICY" velour jumpsuit over her middle-aged-but-still-trying bikini. It's all right, Miss Lady, I'm picking up what you're putting down. You're a divorcee and I've had twenty-five Twisted Teas on my dad's pontoon boat today. Let's hop into your Sebring convertible, head back to the raised ranch you mentioned you were awarded in the divorce, and juuuuuust figure it out. I can't tell you how pleased I was to find that she shaved her forty-five-year-old vagina. I know that wasn't a thing with her generation, so I didn't expect it, but if she's reading this right now, I'd like her to know I appreciated the effort. To this day, she represents the biggest age gap in who I've been with.

Months after that old bag and I had our way with one another, I found out that she has a son named Jared.

He is my age. Weird, right? What's weirder is that upon finding that out, I immediately looked for, found, and friended Jared on Facebook. It has been years, and he hasn't confirmed me yet. Maybe he knows I licked his mom's C-section scar that she was left with after giving birth to him. Do you think he can sense it? Ironically, that scar is why I friended him. I owe him a beer for keeping her slow cooker in pristine shape by opting to take the trapdoor out. Thanks, Jared!

Step 3: Find Your Wheelhouse

You're on a hot streak. You haven't turned down one opportunity. Now you're starting to put some miles on the tires, and you're just plain tired of buying new sheets. It's time to start thinking about narrowing down the playing field a little bit. I am by no means suggesting anyone should ever actively *look* for a relationship, unless your biology is ticking louder than that giant clock at the end of *Hook*. Remember, you can't force or arrange these things, but you can't be a wild mongoose forever, either. I think of it like *American Idol*. On each new season's premiere, they show all the crazy, eccentric nut jobs who are terrible. They're laughable, entertaining, funny, but ultimately have zero chance of making it to the next round. They are there purely for entertainment, for fluff, and for perspective on how good the coming contestants are going to be, comparatively. Then it's time to bring on the real talent and let America vote, God damn it. What's important to remember is you can't do this forever. I think about that all the time. You should only be single long enough to remember why you want to be with someone. Don't forget how nice romance can be. Don't forget how fun the opposite sex can be. I think about it constantly. It's why my go-to answer to any question involving my upcoming weekend plans is "probably just doing some laundry, hanging with Frank, and finding my future wife."

A Coonskin Tale

(Dave)

Coming from upstate New York can mean a lot of things to a lot of people. Those who live in New York City define "upstate" as anything north of themselves. Upstate could be Westchester, Lake Placid, Hudson, Albany, or fucking Buffalo. Mike and I grew up outside Albany, and one of the best parts about it was living with direct access to the Adirondacks.

If you haven't been to the Adirondacks you should probably go. It's untouched by all the crap around it. The Adirondack Park represents a freeze frame in history, when America was the jacked football player at the bar drinking Budweiser, attracting babes, and doing the right thing with his heart of gold. Badass, but still deep. Now America is more like the guy who is four levels drunker than everyone at the bar, is sort of out of shape, won't stop talking, but is actually pretty amusing and a blast to party with. His moves aren't what they used to be, and he dresses like it's the late nineties, but oh hey, he just bought the entire bar a round of shots. Classic move, 2015 America! The Adirondacks, though? We're talking about a big old 6.1 million–acre park that Teddy Roosevelt put aside for us so we wouldn't forget just how far a breath of fresh air goes toward getting a fella back to neutral. You know how people toss around the term "God's country" when they're in a location so beautiful it makes them think they're hanging out with God? That expression comes from the Adirondacks. God owns lakefront property there. I'm not lying to you, guys. When people used to get tuberculosis or the clap or whatever the fuck people got afflicted with way back when, doctors would insist that somebody take 'em up north to the Adirondacks and just air it out.

Rivers, lakes, streams, bridges, golf, moose, maybe the occasional meth lab, but also nature, mountains, bearded men. The ADKs have old pickup trucks, antique stores, and racism. But also bald eagles! They've got it all. I'd like to buy a motorcycle with a sidecar, strap Frank the Bulldog in, and ride around the Adirondacks for days looking at stuff. You can come, too. If you do go to the Adirondacks, just make sure you don't spend much of your time in the southern end of Lake George. They call it "the gateway to the Adirondacks," but really that just translates to the fake and gimmicky Adirondacks. It's the southernmost part of the park, where most people enter, and therefore has the most shit jammed into it. It's not even fun for kids: Olde Tyme photos, shitty mini golf, shitty arcades, guys with classic cars taking laps on the .5 miles of "strip," 3-D movie theaters with rumble chairs that spray water at you, Frankenstein walking around outside of a fucking wax museum. All of that shit, with tetanus or rabies on 90 percent of everything you touch. All you'll find at the southern end of Lake George is cheap bachelorette parties, raunchy boat-up bars, and a whole mess of tourists down from Canada. Also, *tons* of Asians renting boats and wearing tacky orange life vests. It's a good time and a complete shithole all at the same time. Oh, did I mention the southern end of Lake George is exactly where this story takes place?

Way more important than the where is the who. Have I mentioned *The Entertainer* yet? If I haven't, I apologize. He's an important character, even though he's an inanimate object. *The Entertainer* is our dad's twenty-four-foot pontoon boat. It's technically called an "Aqua Patio," which is nautical for *We made a living room fucking FLOAT, you guys! The Entertainer* is made of long couches, lounge chairs, several wooden tables, a carpet, a love seat with a cooler underneath it, and eighty-eight horses of American power to push it around. My parents bought it new in 1988 and it just won't quit. The most people Mike and I ever fit on *The Entertainer* was seventeen fully grown healthy adults, two large-breed dogs, and a full keg of Busch. Regular Busch, not Busch Light. We were nuts to butts on board *The Entertainer* that day; you couldn't see either pontoon coming out of the water. From the distance, I bet it looked like seventeen Jesuses partying on water. Coincidentally, that's how I picture *my* version of Jesus. Party Jesus is so cool, dancing on water and spreading the good news.

Back to *The Entertainer*. The thing has been through

hell! It's twenty-seven years old and has lived the life of five boats. *The Entertainer* and Mike are actually the same age. Both have endured an insane amount of abuse to their bodies and Mike seems to be the only one showing signs of wear and tear. *The Entertainer* is indestructible, reliable, and authentic. It baffles me to hear our folks talk about the glory days when they first bought *The Entertainer* and partied on it harder than we ever would. I thought seventeen dancing Jesuses was a lot, but it doesn't break their record, which still stands to this day. They fit twenty-four people on board. It doesn't seem possible, but for some reason I believe them. When we had seventeen dancing Jesuses on board, I can distinctly remember thinking that if the smallest fish in the lake farts right now, we're all fucked. Twenty-four people? They tell it like they didn't even bat an eye.

Maybe the pontoons were more buoyant back then. Maybe they were sick fucks like Mike and I are, and they actively tried to sink it. Between my folks, their friends, and then later a degenerate band of Stangle brothers and their buddies, *The Entertainer* has proved completely unsinkable. No seaworthy vessel has survived more troublemaking white folks since the *Mayflower*. The thing just won't die. It reminds me of Inigo Montoya from *The Princess Bride*. Remember at the end when Christopher Guest just keeps stabbing him all over the place, but Montoya won't quit, because he needs to avenge his father? *The Entertainer* is like that, applied to drinking.

Despite the boat's advanced age, I would actually

argue that *The Entertainer* has peaked in the last five years. It's rare to see an old-school pontoon out on the water anymore, let alone an unsinkable BEAST with eighties lettering and more than two decades of Lake George registration stickers proudly displayed across the bow like an arm-sleeve tattoo. That makes *The Entertainer* recognizable everywhere it goes. One time years ago, the Warren County Sheriff's Department had put an APB out on it. My dad and his buddies were fishing and got pulled over by a police boat. It turns out the APB was because the police wanted to borrow it for a parade, but they didn't know who owned it. They figured they'd pull it over the next time it was spotted, so the cop could ask the favor. Yes, it's been in several parades now. Show me another boat with a more impressive party resume besides maybe, *maybe*, the Beatles' Yellow Submarine.

• • •

One Fourth of July a few years back, some buddies, Mike, and I took *The Entertainer* out on Lake George all day. You know that southern end I was talking about? That is where most of this story will eventually take place, but for most of the day, we were bopping around miles north of there, from bay to bay. Upstate folks will recognize the landmarks by experience, but they're all aptly named, anyway. First we hit Log Bay (the one with logs lining the bottom), then Sandy Bay (the one with sand on the bottom), and then Paradise Bay (the one with loose women everywhere). At the time, I was twenty-five, fresh off a nice dump (by Nancy, not my butthole) and in a really sick phase of my life. I was playing host on *The Entertainer* all afternoon, and I've got to tell you, it was tough. I was one of eleven people, eight of whom were coupled off. The remainder were male buddies. If you were wondering, (twenty-one-year-old) Mike had a (twenty-one-year-old) girlfriend at the time. She was awful, but she was an absolute babe. So shallow, Mike. I don't know how my friends pulled this off, but at the time, every single one of their girlfriends was a real knockout. Good for us, we peaked!

What did this translate to? Basically, all I was doing all day was driving people around on a boat while looking at girls in bikinis. And drinking. People were cupcaking left and right. My buddy Nick was getting a hand job while floating under the anchored *Entertainer*. Although that sounds extremely difficult from a logistical standpoint, it can happen. Fact is, the very idea of everyone being so sexual around me was driving me nuts. It was fucking torture. You know how I feel about bikinis, you guys. Hey, everyone, let's go to Log Bay and tie up with a bunch of other boats that are DRIPPING with bikini-clad women. *Oh, Dave, are you putting a shirt on so you can hide the tip of your dick when you tuck your boner in?* (Power move.) *No problem!* I drank slowly to stay in control and help escort everyone around. That isn't like me, since *The Entertainer* practically drives itself . . . but it was the Fourth, guys. I wanted to honor our forefathers with some responsibility.

By the time an afternoon of day drinking turned into happy hour, and happy hour turned into everyone in the gang getting gussied up to hit the town for the night, everyone had gotten their sexual thrills out of their system. Except for me. A man can only be in such an environment for so long before his carnal nature takes over. Mike and the guys with the girlfriends had brought sand to the beach, so they were all set. My other single friends had branched off with those they met during the day. They were laying groundwork, at least. Me? I was right where I left off. Captain Dave, president of the boner club. I was running hot. Real hot. I didn't know what to do. I started acting funny. It was as if I couldn't hide how horny I was. I was a dog in heat. The sexuality was seeping out of my pores. Women around me were disgusted, alarmed, somehow flattered, and intrigued all at the same time.

I wanted to have a little Dave time, frost my belly button if you know what I mean; that would have been the natural move to take myself down from dangerously horny to reasonably horny, but I kept getting interrupted. Tried to JO on the boat, but it was too open, people kept walking up. Tried to JO in the bathroom, but girls kept knocking on the door. Tried to JO in the water even, but that just wasn't working. Ever tried it? It's hard having sex in the water, and even harder without a vagina in the mix. Drinking was plan B and also plan A. I suppressed my horniness the way a twenty-five-year-old male properly deals with any issue—by drinking until I temporarily forgot about it. While doing so, and while everyone else was still cupcaking with their gals, I was getting weird.

At some point, we had befriended strangers and docked at their lake house, where I found a Davy Crockett raccoon hat. Those hats are pretty on point. Why do you think it was one of the most historic bad boys in American history who put them on the map? Why do you think no one has been able to pull one off since? Maybe because no one can combine fashion with frontier pioneering quite like Davy Crockett did. Davy was close to something, but he wasn't thinking far enough outside of the box. After some toying, I tucked it into the seat of my pants, in a way that suggested that I had myself a raccoon tail. *Boom!* At that moment, an incredible gimmick was born. I really pulled it off, too. I was born to have a tail. It absolutely killed with the lake house crowd. Everyone needed to talk about it, everyone needed to ask about it, many wanted to touch it. I let them. "Just please, don't tug." I developed a repertoire, where I explained that I was born with a tail and my parents declined to have it removed at birth. After a few years, when it was growing at a faster rate than predicted (I would later change it to "hairier"), doctors told my parents it was part of my spine and that they risked certain paralysis if they attempted surgery. The decision practically made itself—I *had* to go out with this thing on tonight. The only problem was my sobriety. It was gone. It was the last one to leave the party, and it turned the lights off on the way out.

We had a big van, and we were going to drive to a few bars in a town up the road, but there was no way anyone could drive at that point. I was the last one to start drinking and coon-tail-mania got me all antsy in my pantsy. I was already wobbly from unsuccessfully trying to drown out my horniness. It left me aroused, tailed, and *drunk*. I couldn't drive a car, no one could . . . but we did have *The Entertainer*. Hell yes! It was like a lightbulb went off in my head. I don't want to be seen at the *cool* bars with a raccoon tail, anyway. I've got a gimmick going, and I want to use it on fellow sickos who would appreciate it. I was the raccoon tail guy; I'll drive the shit out of that boat! Southern Lake George, here we come.

If you want to have a raunchy time in Lake George, you go to one bar and one bar only—Christie's On The Lake. That's where people go to get wet, and not with lake water. When you pull up to a waterfront bar on an overflowing pontoon boat blasting Boy George, people turn their heads to see what they are dealing with. That's exactly what the scene was by the time we got there. We were tuned up and we made an entrance that went further than I could have imagined. What happened next was as if the gods looked down upon me and decided to conduct an experiment to see how much pleasure the horniest guy in the world could possibly get from a best-case scenario falling into his hands—and whether he could survive this without a heart attack. We had been at Christie's for just one drink before she approached me. She was one of the most beautiful women I have ever seen. She was short (which I typically don't go for) and had funky blond hair (which I always go for). She was dressed differently than most of the gals there. She was wearing exclusively skintight denim and not much of it. She was putting out one cigarette as she lit her next. She was moving, shaking, and picture taking. Everything she did looked attractive to me. It was as if she was approaching me for an hour as I watched her move closer. The real kicker? On top of everything, she was French. Jackpot. Maybe she was French-Canadian, but I stuck with believing she was a purebred Frenchy, because it was sexier in my head. Canucks are cool, but not for this story. Her accent was blowing me away.

As I was halfway through my first drink, she approached me from across the bar and introduced herself. I loved how forward she was. Her name was Lisa L'Poop. Yup. Lisa L'Poop. I swear to God that is what she said when she introduced herself. *Hello, I am Lisa L'Poop.* I'm sorry, did you say Lisa . . . L'Poop? She had a little French accent that somehow made L'Poop sound sexy. Not if you say it like I would say it. I would say it "LAH POOP." She said it way cooler and quicker, like *LEH-POO'b*. I don't know why, but for some reason typing it in a smaller italic font with a silent *b* made me think it reads more like she said it. *Tricky French people.* How do they do that? *Yes, Lisa L'Poop.* She asked, *How do you do?* No one else had ever asked me how do I do, because it wasn't 1952, so I was of course taken aback by her. It didn't take me long to fuck things up. The second I opened my mouth to say something, things went south. I couldn't have sounded like a fatter, duller American dude. *I'M DAV . . . IDOff.* That's what I said. It was as if all of a sudden, halfway through saying the name I've had, oh, I don't know, my entire life, I decided that Dave was the stupidest name in history and I needed something sexier to counter L'Poop. I also made this decision while I was halfway through saying "Dave," so I had already committed to the first syllable. Lisa L'Poop didn't miss a beat, though. *Very nice to meet you, eh, Davidoff? Please do tell me about this tail?* Holy shit. What? The tail! I forgot about the tail. In fact, while I was busy embarrassing myself, I had forgotten altogether how incredibly pent-up I was in the first place. Now it all came rushing back to me. I'm shitfaced in a bar wearing a coonskin tail, fighting off a libido that will *not* cool out, and I'm talking to a once-in-a-lifetime babe who somehow hasn't walked away after the worst introduction in the history of the United States.

You can't fall off the floor, right? It was time to pick myself up and see where I could take this. As it turns out, pretty goddamn far. L'Poop and I hit it off big-time. We exchanged pleasantries until we finished our drinks, then I bought us another round. I would joke, she'd laugh even though the joke went over her head. She'd say something in French, I'd laugh because I'm not sophisticated enough to understand her. The tail jokes were incredibly successful, though. Every one was a home run. I couldn't believe how well it was going. I actually *couldn't* believe it, though—as in, it was going so well I thought she might be a hooker or something. All of these paranoid thoughts started going through my head, like what if my friends had found this chick and put her up to it, because they knew how desperate I was? I thought maybe I was being messed with. Those feelings temporarily subsided when we began Frenching before we even finished our second drink! That's right! I'm talking full-on smooching in the middle of the bar, Davidoff and L'Poop, within ten minutes of meeting each other. I was grabbing her butt, she was grabbing my tail, it was magic. Mike was twenty feet away from me, hootin' and hollerin' at me with my friends, like a pack of dogs.

The DJ must have even been in my corner, because we made out for at least three Usher songs in a row before she whispered that we should step outside. *For a cigarette?* I asked her. I must have come off so boyish and dopey. What was she doing with me? I sounded like Eeyore from *Winnie-the-Pooh*. *Eh, somezing like that?* she said with a cute little smile. Okay what the FUCK is going on here? Did someone seriously put her up to this? It was all somehow working. We walked out of the bar, fingers interlaced like we'd been dating for all four years of high school, and the bouncer gave me this huge grin like, "Didn't I just see you come in here like . . . twelve minutes ago?" I gave him the cool-guy nod back, naturally. L'Poop and I got outside and she started kissing me *again*. I didn't even get a cigarette, which was probably a godsend, because with the way things were going, I would have taken one dorky pull off it and erupted in a fit of coughing as she took a long, slow, smooth pull and blew smoke rings that morphed into the shape of hearts. No butts, though; at least not the smoking ones. We started to get pretty handsy outside the bar. *I want you to take me out of here, Davidoff.* Come on. Really? I mean, I will, but really? I had to be getting played here. I'm not going to say that Lake George is overflowing with eligible and desirable bachelors, but why me?

I evaluated my options. *The Entertainer* was a no-go; it was in plain sight down on the docks, so the entire world would see. Not that I'm opposed to that sort of thing; just wait for our chapter on that. There was a hotel not far from Christie's, but my credit card was still inside at the bar being maxed out by Mike and the gang. L'Poop was staying in another hotel right next door to Christie's, but it was occupied by friends who got too much sun that day. With no plan at all, L'Poop and I started walking south. At this point, we were only looking for privacy. After about ninety quick make-out breaks with L'Poop whispering in ol' Davidoff's ear about how sexy he was (note to self: MOVE TO FRANCE) we found ourselves in front of Fort William Henry. I could go into a whole history lesson on just what Fort William Henry is, but this isn't a history book. All you need to know is that it's a British fort on the southern end of Lake George best known for the notorious atrocities committed by Indians against surrendered British troops following a successful French siege in 1757. Ever see *The Last of the Mohicans*?

That's where all that shit took place. On the vast front lawn of Fort William Henry, there is a statue. I'm not sure who the statue is of. I'd assume it's of William Henry. I'm also not sure who William Henry even was. He was probably tortured by those savage Indians. What I do know is that William Henry's statue is like a playground made of marble and L'Poop was getting downright freaky with me on it. She was taking her clothes off and giggling, which is possibly the hottest combination of two things a French chick could do, as we chased each other around the statue. I imagine if Martians were observing Earth at that very moment and saw the two of us—one goofy, uncoordinated white guy chasing around a gorgeous giggling French gal—they probably wrote in their Martian notebooks *Note to Self: MOVE TO EARTH*.

Soon things started to get hot and heavy and ol' William Henry wasn't the only guy sporting some marble. As perfect as this was about to be, I was still freaking out like something was wrong. It didn't add up. Was this girl about to drug me and steal my organs? That was the honest-to-God thought that was going on in my head as she wrapped her legs around me. Well, that thought went away pretty quickly, within about three to five seconds. I thought I was enjoying it so much that I was imagining fireworks in the background. Then I remembered it was the Fourth of July. An American slob making love to a French 10 on the Fourth of July on top of a statue of a guy who was tortured by Indians. For my money, it doesn't get any more American than that, folks.

We finished and smoked cigarettes as we lay ass-naked, half on the grass and half on the statue. L'Poop and I eventually gathered up the clothes we had been tearing off each other and wandered back toward the bar scene. I had a shirt on, though I was not sure it was mine, and definitely didn't find my boxers. I didn't even know what else I was missing, only that I was decent enough to pass the no shirt/no shoes/no service test. Since we had left the bar so early together, things were still raging as we got back to Christie's. L'Poop told me she was going to pop into her hotel room next door to freshen up. *We'd better exchange numbers now; I don't want to lose track of you.* It was the smoothest thing I had said all night. *Absolutely not,* she responded, deadpan. Then she smiled, walked into the hotel lobby, and I never saw her again. She never came back to the bar, I couldn't find her at any other bars, and the hotel night manager assured me there was no LAH POOP staying at his hotel. What's worse? No one except the bouncer even saw me leave the bar with her. I came back to a crowd of drunken friends yelling at me for flaking out on them. When I told Mike the story, he laughed me off as if it never could have happened. I didn't fight him on it; what was the point? I was happy to be back there with all my organs still inside my body and all my demons outside of it, finally.

The night ended how most nights like that ended back then, in a complete blackout. When I pulled myself together the next day, I got *The Entertainer* out of the water and onto the trailer, loaded up my friends, and began to head home. The drive out of Lake George the day after is always depressing. You drive past all the things you still want to be doing, then watch them fade into the rearview mirror. The last landmark you drive by on your way out of town is Fort William Henry. As I looked into my rearview to bid adieu to one of the wilder and luckier nights I'd had, I caught a glimpse of that statue of William Henry. Someone had found the coonskin hat nearby and put it on his head. I'll always remember you, Lisa L'Poop.

It's All About the Nipple

Young Man, Count Your Titty Blessings

(Mike)

The older fellas I know love talking about how much technology has changed the flirting game between their generation and mine. Once upon a time, they were just like me. They were in their twenties, young professionals, living in a bustling city filled with women. The major difference between chasing women then and chasing women now? Technology. When they were our age, the concept of a gal being willing *and* able to take a sexy picture of herself and then instantly send it to a fella she was sweating was absolutely bonkers. All a gal needs to do nowadays is pop off some clothes, do the skinny-arm pose (hand on hip, ladies!), kissy-face those lips, and snap. Some lucky guy has a little red number 1 in the corner of his Snapchat and the games have begun. We men take for granted how easy that process is.

Picture the entire operation if you limit yourself to the technology of previous generations. I'm not just saying before Snapchat, but before camera phones, digital cameras, before everyone had a Dell desktop computer riddled with viruses. I'm talking about a time when the phrase "nudie shot" would make people think of the Hooters drink menu. Back then, it was so much more than point, snap, and send. Imagine trying to replicate that with limited technology? I imagine a young, plucky gal named Sue asking her older friend Peggy to borrow her camera, because younger people can't afford cameras. So she goes to Peggy's apartment at a time they designated to meet hours earlier, while in the same company, because no one had cell phones to make last-minute plans. Then she lugs the camera in the over-the-shoulder case to the local pharmacy and buys a roll of film. Then she goes back to her apartment and puts the film in the camera, but she forgot to get batteries. So she goes back to the pharmacy and gets batteries, but they're the wrong kind. She wasn't even paying attention, because she had gotten a little high at her apartment while loading the film. Once she gets the film set and the right batteries, she gets the camera on and uses the entire roll of film taking nudie shots of herself. Selfies, mirror shots, full bush everywhere. There is probably an Andy Warhol print in the background of some of them. She has to take a ton of them, because she can't see whether they are good or bad as she takes them. Then she has to get the film developed, but she doesn't want to go to her local pharmacy. They are pictures of her naked, and that shit is unheard-of. Plus, she's already been in there three times for film and batteries, and the guy who works there is sort of creepy. So she goes to the weird pharmacy, the one up in Morningside Heights. But film development isn't instant; in fact, it takes a fucking day. You have to drop it off and then come back the next day to pick it up. Then she remembers the new thing that some places have called one-hour photos. How much of a technological mind blower that is! But only the nice places have it, like the place she's already been to three times. She really likes the guy she took the pictures for, plus, she already put so much time and effort into the whole thing, so she might as well see it through.

She goes back to the original pharmacy that she's already been to three times and goes to the one-hour photo counter. The guy behind the counter is creepy and it skeeves her out to think he'll be developing her pictures, but then again she's already in this deep, so she might as well keep going. He says it will take an hour, so she goes and gets a coffee, then buys an envelope and a few stamps. When she goes to pick up the pictures, the creepy guy is looking at her even creepier and the envelope he gives her only has twenty-one pictures in it, even though there should be twenty-four. She doesn't argue with him, because there is an old lady behind her in the store who reminds her of her grandmother. So instead, she just hopes he didn't take the best three and walks home. Then she has to comb through and pick out the best one. She puts it in an envelope, writes the guy's address on it, pops two stamps on it (to *really* make sure it gets there), walks down her stairs, out her door, down the block, and drops it in the mailbox. Then, two to three business days later, he receives a nudie shot. Nice!

Since the older fellas I know won't let me forget how much technology has changed everything between our generations, it makes me think about how I will give the next generation of young men, and anyone who will even still listen to me at that point, a bunch of shit about how great they have it. Most dads or grandads use the ol' *when I was your age I had to walk to school, ten miles in the snow, uphill, both ways!* That one is so dumb. Hey, baby boomers—of all the luxuries our generation has been afforded over yours, school transportation is your go-to? Not even a mention of the invention of Google Maps or the prevalence of gals shaving their boxes? We shouldn't let our generation's equivalent example be as lame for the next batch of youngsters. The difference between my generation and theirs is already showing its incredibly sexy head. I've got cousins, ten and twelve years old, these two little punks. I think about how they'll have it easier than I did and in what areas. How about the almighty boob? When I was in my adolescence, all I wanted was to up my boobie count. We weren't seeing live boobs in person, maybe a nipple slip here or there. For the most part, we had to rely on the TV. You could rent an R-rated movie, but that wasn't a guarantee there would be a boob in it. Plus, our parents weren't too big on letting us watch R movies. That didn't stop us, but we weren't going to put all our efforts into acquiring an R movie if we weren't sure it would deliver. You had to be sure. Forget looking it up on the Internet to confirm; Al Gore hadn't invented it yet. To find out where all the boobies were at, you had to hit the streets and do your research. You had to check in with the kids who lived in a one-parent home on the other side of the tracks. They were watching all the R movies; they had the scoop. You had to keep your ear to the ground. I can remember one time I was at one of my soccer games, waiting for it to start. I didn't have to warm up or stretch or anything, because I was our team's goalie. I was six feet four at twelve years old, guarding a seven-foot goal. Good luck scoring, normal-sized twelve-year-olds. Instead, I hung out with the refs—they were local high school kids paid seven dollars a game to blow the whistle when the ball went out of bounds. Later on in my life, I would become one of those refs for part-time work. I was eventually not welcomed back, because I gave a red card to any parent who argued a call.

One Saturday morning before a game, I can remember this one older ref Andy talking about a movie that had just gone from theaters to VHS. I can still remember it was called *Fair Game*. It was your classic nineties blockbuster. William Baldwin played Max Kirkpatrick, a cop who protects Kate McQuean (played by Cindy Crawford, hello!), a civil law attorney on the run from a renegade KGB team out to get her. Andy confirmed that you see Cindy Crawford's boobs during a steamy sex scene that took place on a moving freight train. Like I said, classic nineties blockbuster. I was ecstatic! A name as big as Cindy Crawford, showing boob!? The hunt was on! I was like a teenage girl hearing about a confirmed sighting of Justin Timberlake. I was *on it*. My best hope was to hit up Blockbuster (RIP) and rent the VHS. There was no way Mama Stangle would let me pop an R movie into the cart; she had strict rules when it came to that. Naturally, my workaround was having my old man take me to Blockbuster. He had no idea how Blockbuster even worked. He might not have even known what it was. He isn't too big on movies. The only movie he ever liked is *Blazing Saddles,* because racism is funny and acceptable in that one. All he cared to know about Blockbuster was that a visit kept us kids busy all weekend. I grabbed a copy of *Fair Game* from the new releases section, a few other assorted titles that would act as buffers as I waited for my folks to nod off, and a big box of Butterfinger BBs—'cause I was a fucking baller.

I saw Cindy Crawford's boobies that night, my friends. I saw them loud and I saw them clear. I still remember them, and that train scene. Quick note: there were KGB operatives actively shooting machine guns everywhere, while William was dogging Cindy out on a warehouse crate. You just can't suppress a man's carnal desires. On that same note, think of all the effort I put into seeing that set of boobs. It was a grassroots operation. Literally, that soccer field was grassy as shit. It involved eavesdropping, car rides, throwing Denny off my scent, and hours of buffer tapes until I knew I wouldn't be interrupted. Now, imagine the same process today? Our pops complained about trekking to school ten miles in the snow? Try playing a wimp sport like soccer, *every* Saturday, just to get the lowdown on where all the smut is. *Then* you start your trek, and Blockbuster is way farther away than school is, amigo. My punk little cousins? They've both got iPhones. You don't think they know how to enable private browsing? One click. Titties on the playground. Titties at lunch. Titties during the seventh-inning stretch. These kids are probably looking at nipples while they're brushing their teeth, one-handed style. It's tit city for kids today. After I saw my first pair of boobs, it was *months* before I realized they weren't all the same. Wait, nipples are different!? Imagine if my first one was pierced or a jujube nipple? I'd be scarred! Now kids are trading nipple pics like they're pogs. They probably only remember what a nipple looks like for twenty-five seconds, until the next one comes along. So fast-forward a few generations to me on a porch in a rocking chair, old and weathered, and I won't be scolding my little punk grandkids about some tough walk to school. I'll be telling them to count their titty blessings, 'cause they don't know what rough *is*.

Extended Pleasure

I Just Can't Sex Right!

(Mike)

Ever been intimidated by the prospect of making love to a pretty gal? That was college for me, from day one. I couldn't even come close to a hookup without complete intimidation. College was the first time I'd ever been single and sexually active at the same time. I'd had a girlfriend throughout all of high school, since the first day my peener moved until I got to college. Back then, that was the only way to have any sort of consistent sex: you had to be *with* someone. No one was having one-night stands, and if they were, you really had to work at them or get lucky after you split a sixer of Smirnoff Ice. When I got to college and was a single fella, there were a lot of new things in my sexual game. There were a lot of firsts, a lot of lasts, and a lot of one-time-onlys. By the time I got to my junior year at the State University of New York at Oswego, I was really starting to hit my stride. I was in decent shape, had that cool-guy house all the cool guys have right near the bars, and had a real hard-body group of friends. We were very Abercrombie & Fitch, just walking around in jeans with no shirts, for no reason.

If you spotted me back then, chances are you'd see a combination of a backward hat, a Jeep Wrangler, a Frisbee, and American flags everywhere. I can go on. Crazy sunglasses, shitty rap, patchy facial hair, going to mixers with the rugby guys. You name it! I was finally cool! I was "so college," and loving it.

It was right about this time that I was gaining some confidence with the fairer sex. Have you ever seen those signs outside factories that say IT HAS BEEN 64 DAYS SINCE OUR LAST ACCIDENT? They just keep adding another day on that red number to let everyone know how safe they are. It had been sixty-four days since my last really embarrassing sexual encounter. For my factory, that was a record! Confidence was high, sexual morale was trending upward, and I was feeling good. It was right about this time that I met Team Player. Team Player and I are in touch to this very day. She's a great gal. When she found out about this book, she made me swear I wouldn't write about her. Yeah, right! Come on! This story isn't even your fault, TP. Everything else was, though.

Team Player was a little sexpot. She was a sultry five feet two, DD, freckled shoulders, strawberry blonde smoldering temptress. She was really something. TP was *way* out of my league, and a year older, too. Bonus points on that one. I had known TP for a few months and been into her for exactly that long. I knew she thought I was at least cute, maybe because there was such a height differential between us that she couldn't really see the details of my face? I always get a bump from short girls, and I never understood why. They are basically just looking up my nostrils. I'll take it, though.

I had been working on a slow play with TP since day one. A night came when we were together and I was just feeling it. For one reason or another, I had a good showing when we were together at a bar that night. Maybe I was wearing a cool shirt or she saw me yucking it up with the bouncer? Maybe I had just trimmed my nose hairs and she noticed? Who knows. Somehow I impressed her enough to put it out there that I thought she was just swell and I'd like to set up a second (*sober*) meeting a couple of nights later. She agreed! People don't go on dates in college; that's just ridiculous. What was a sober meet-up? It was a school night, and she wanted to watch a movie . . . and you know what that means. I was in like Flynn! The only problem was I hadn't had sober sex in months. It was college! If you're single, when is the last time you had a 100 percent sober sexual encounter with someone brand-new? If it was recently, I'm jealous. If you pulled this off in college, I'm green with envy! Most sex outside of a relationship is drunk, especially in college. I'm supposed to work up the balls to perform without a buzz on? Are you nuts? If I had sex sober, I tended to think about things too much. I'd finish too quick, I'd get too concerned about how it was for her, or I'd become distracted by things in my room that I never noticed before, because I had always been drunk. *Hey, when did I get a cactus?* Drunk sex just took all of that off the table. It didn't afford me the opportunity to overthink it. Now I was facing the Mount Everest of sober sex. TP was totally and completely sexually intimidating. What could I do? I was a goner if I didn't come up with a game plan. Christ, don't panic. What are my options?

First, use a condom! Safety first. That's always my motto. Well, that's always my sexual motto, anyway. I actually don't apply it to anything else in my life. In fact, I sort of disregard it if we aren't talking about my penis. People protect what they naturally love. I don't have a son. I don't have a dog. My penis is all I've got. So I went to the condom store: Walmart. After a ten-minute distraction in the frozen pizza section (happens to the best of us) I made my way over to the condom area with a couple of DiGiornos in tow. The condom section isn't really that big compared to something like the snack aisle, the shampoo section, or even the frozen pizza section. People spread out when shopping for those items, because there are so many options. You can fit all the condom options on one five-foot shelf, top to bottom. This makes everyone shuffle into one spot, shoulder to shoulder. Guys give each other nods and looks like *Yeeaah buddy, you, too? All right!* Gals? They just circle the section and pretend to be shopping for tampons or something until the coast is clear.

After exchanging knowing glances with the fellas around me, I started to browse through my options. Textured, tantric, ultrathin, shared pleasure, flavored (cool!), glow in the dark (whaaat!?), spermicide (gross!).

Naturally, I had my sights set on some lambskin condoms, because lambskin is classy and gals like luxury. That was, until I noticed a pack that said *extended pleasure* written across the box like a fucking Lite-Brite. I was so intrigued. Could this be the answer to my prayers? Extending our pleasure was literally the exact goal I was looking to achieve. I was saved! I did a quick read of the information on the box, none of which I actually paid any attention to, and I was sold.

Team Player was waiting for me at my place (ballsy move, love it) and looking foxy. She had the comfortable Sunday casual look down like you wouldn't believe. Dresses, bikinis, tank tops—those are easy to make look sexy. You just put your boobs into the fabric that holds the boobs, and BAM! Fellas be staring. But when you can make your lying-around look turn some heads, you've really got it going on. Team Player had it going on. She was definitely wearing that Victoria's Secret body spray all the gals were wearing back then. Where do I sign?

I popped a DVD into my laptop to get movie night started. *The Lion King.* It was Dave's go-to movie to watch with a gal when he was in college. I will neither justify nor defend this move. Say what you will about his tactics, but it *works*. I don't think Rafiki had even held newborn Simba up for all of the animal kingdom to behold before Team Player and I started doing some serious necking. I was so confident with my purchase that all of that sexual anxiety had gone right out the window. I was a champ! We were about to have some extendedly pleasurable coitus. Flip the factory sign to 65, folks! I started really putting some moves on her. We took our time; I guess you do that during sober sex. We did some hand stuff. We warmed up. We got the blood flowing. It was nice. Soon, we were ready for extended pleasure.

Is there any more vulnerable moment a man can have than when he is putting a condom on? The act of putting a rubber on is just so unnatural. It creates a really annoying break in the romance, plus, they are smelly! I always feel like the gal is looking over my shoulder, judging my technique or something. I did the best a man could do to maintain sexual flow while seamlessly fitting a piece of latex around his dick. I thought I had done a pretty good job on all fronts, but once this extended pleasure condom was on, I *instantly* knew something was wrong.

Very wrong! Oh my God, just writing this is taking me back there! What was happening? What was this feeling? The condom was . . . what was it doing? What is this? No! It was making my wiener go numb! NUMB. As in zero feeling. Think about when you get Novocain at the dentist, and you can't really talk because your mouth is numb, so you just spit and drool instead of forming real words. What if that happened right before you had to give an important speech? That was what was happening with my penis! My penis all of a sudden became a stuttering King George VI addressing the British at Wembley!

Set the sign back to o DAYS SINCE OUR LAST ACCI-

DENT. I hadn't thought this whole "extended pleasure" thing through. You guys probably picked up on that at least a few paragraphs ago, right? Well, I didn't, because I was an idiot, okay? I was panicking; extended pleasure, how did I get the interpretation so wrong? How did I just instantly believe that if I wore *this* particular condom I would just last a long time and everything would be great? Sex wasn't a cell phone contract I could just extend. Wear this condom for unlimited nights and weekends! So what does "extended pleasure" really mean? Oh, let me tell you, the condom company just coats the inside of these bad boys with fucking Novocain! When marketers say, "There's a sucker born every minute," they are 100 percent referring to Mike Stangle buying condoms in a Walmart while distracted by a combination of sexual anxiety and frozen pizzas. Okay, deep breath, Mike. Assess the situation. My dick was completely numb, but somehow still hard. This was a blessing. Considering my past luck, I just automatically assumed numbness meant I would very quickly go soft. No need to totally panic—ah shit, now it went soft, too. Panic! Sexual anxiety combined with Novocain? I didn't stand a chance. Plus, by this point, Mufasa had just been stampeded by a herd of wildebeests. Shit was hitting the fan.

It didn't take long for Team Player to pick up on the problem. She knew something was going on, and it didn't take her long to ask about it. How was I supposed to explain? No way. I was silent. At first, she was concerned it was something she did. That always surprised me about gals, that when a guy can't perform, the gal immediately thinks it was something she did? Little hint for you ladies: It's *never* something you did. Gals don't make boners go away, ever. Typically, if it isn't because we wore a DICK-NUMBING PIECE OF LATEX THAT TRICKED US, it's some other problem with us, so keep your head up. I assured Team Player it wasn't her fault at all, then scampered and quickly did a fake look at the condom package and pulled something like an *Ohhh shit, these are extended pleasure? What the hell? Must have grabbed the wrong pack at the store* move. It was my only option.

I quickly boiled it down for her, and to her credit and my surprise, she didn't waste a second trying to right this wrong. She was there to help, and she made that clear. As if my penis were drowning and my balls contained oxygen, Team Player (aptly named now, right?!) ripped that penis sheath from hell off me and immediately began the rescue effort. As her head disappeared below my twin comforter I thought, *Okay, we are at least addressing the problem now. We can get through this together.* It felt nice. It felt real nice. Actually, wait a minute, it was working! Whatever she did down there helped a ton. At first I couldn't feel it at all, but I think my brain, penis, and heart all got together on one end of the tug-of-war against Novocain and collectively yelled "Heave!" I was getting harder, then getting feeling back—the Novocain was wearing off! After just a few minutes, I was up and running. The flag was raised to full mast and patriotically blowing in the breeze. God Bless America!

TP came back upstairs and we got back into our horizontal no-pants dance. At this point, we got rid of the condom plan altogether. I certainly wasn't complaining. The next few minutes were a total roller coaster! Ups, downs, upside downs, screams! It seemed that after all this nonsense, the stars had finally aligned and all was right in the world. We were sexing! And it was fun. I discovered she was a dirty talker. That is such a huge plus, ladies. Man, do I love dirty talk. I was getting really into everything she was saying, and as time went on, the things she was saying got saltier, dirtier, and even sort of nonsensical. Soon I couldn't even understand what she was saying! Wait, was this some sort of advanced-level stuff that I was now hearing for the first time and having trouble keeping up with? It was like a mix of a whisper and slur, but there was a decent amount of lip sounds incorporated. I wasn't going to miss out on this. I decided to mix the position up to get a better listen. The position switch gave me a good look at her face, and that tipped me off that something wasn't quite right.

Her lips looked like Bubba's lips in *Forrest Gump*. Had she been on the army base in Vietnam, Lieutenant Dan would warn her to tuck it in or else she'd get it caught on a tripwire. As I contemplated whether she was having a stroke, I realized just what was happening. When TP was downtown resurrecting my penis, she was really just sucking all the Novocain into her mouth, tongue, cheeks, and throat. There was drool everywhere. The craziest part, which at first seemed like a saving grace but ended up backfiring, was that it did not deter her at all! It was a total circus. That's a huge difference between guys and gals. If a guy starts uncontrollably drooling and slurring his words beyond recognition, no gal will continue to have sex. You'd stop and ask just what the hell is going on. Guys just keep on humping. Once we start, the only three things that will stop us are the words "Stop," "My dad is home!," and "I'm a man." Technically, I can't know for sure if she said any of those words, because she couldn't fucking talk, but her enthusiasm reassured this dog that he should keep on having his day.

While all this was going on, I hadn't even considered my roommates. No one was home when Team Player had come over, so no one knew I had a girl in my room at all. I was living with six other guys at the time, and they were some real sickos. A coupla booze-baggin', no-conscience-havin', dope-smokin' scumbags. My best friends! These guys got home sometime between my initial panic and TP's role as a Rescue Ranger. I could hear the boys hanging in my living room, just one door away.

As my buddies sat outside my bedroom, TP continued to bring the heat. Not only did she not miss a beat physically, but also she continued to try to talk dirty, despite not being able to form any understandable words. This girl was on top of me, giving maximum effort, and drooling on me like a bloodhound. If any of you fellas are asking yourself why I didn't just flip into missionary and take control of the situation—don't you know how Jimi Hendrix died, choking on his own vomit? I was afraid that I was experiencing a close cousin of this exact scenario. What if she was on her back and couldn't feel the saliva accumulating in the back of her throat until it was too late? No way, guys, I can't afford a lawyer! We were already living on the edge with no rubber. I wasn't going to take any more risks. I was perfectly happy with her on top and me on the bottom, where I could serve as sex partner, observer, and lifeguard. Just Mike and gravity, working together, trying to hang on until the end.

Soon, through the paper-thin walls of my college crack house, all my roommates began to hear the noises. They muted the TV and their curiosity grew even more. They moved from the couch toward the wall, and then toward my door. They were perplexed and confused by what they heard. What did the evidence suggest? It seemed to them as though Mike was in his room and he was having sex. Cool! They high-fived in my honor and continued to listen like the sexual deviants they all were. Who is Stangle having sex with in there? What is that sound? Wait, is he? She sounds like some sort of . . . a retarded girl? And what's that in the background? Are they watching *The Lion King*? Is Mike in there taking advantage of a special needs child!? If so, what the hell? They were genuinely concerned! Some were impressed, the sickos. I immediately started hearing the hooting, the hollering, the off-color jokes made loud enough to be sure I could hear. They had no idea! Sex with a special-needs gal would have been a lazy Sunday afternoon compared to what I'd just gone through.

Considering the circumstances, the sex was actually pretty great. After all of this anxiety, Team Player's drool face actually helped me get over my original fears/intimidations. It was like the Novocain from the condom knocked her down a peg in my fantasy draft, and I was able to relax, connect, and have some fun with this drooling-and-babbling bombshell. We were able to have a good laugh about it once the dust had settled. As an added bonus, with her help I was able to convince my roommates not to call the police.

Team Player didn't end up being my girlfriend. We didn't even really end up "dating," exclusively speaking. What we did have was one of those classic college-fling-type situations. Yeah, my counter went back to zero days, but so what! From this disaster forward, Team Player and I had an incredibly honest, open "friendship" (college-style). Yes, we each humiliated ourselves at different points in our roller-coaster ride of a sexual encounter—but yes, we could relax around each other, because we'd seen each other at our worst.

Inside the Sicko's Studio

Mike's Live-Time Notes of Dave's
Most Recent Sexual Encounter

(Mike)

One time when Dave and I got Craigslist-famous for a week and people were actually paying attention to us, we got into some real weird shit. If you go viral, you're automatically playing with house money. Don't waste it. When the next viral craze breaks two days later, and you have to go back to being a normal person, you're going to regret not taking advantage of all the eyes on you. Me and Dave? We got downright silly. We went looking for trouble and found it. A lot of crazy shit started to happen all at once. How many times have you thought of a brilliant idea, only to later forget it because the brain cells previously allocated to remembering it had to be reassigned to keeping a bunch of Twisted Teas at bay? We found the best way to remember an idea to expand on is the "notes" folder in our iPhones—which you can share, by the way. Welcome to 2015, motherfuckers! It is *sick*! In fact, I'm writing this from our notes folder right now. I'm on the subway, I've got no service, I'm listening to John Mayer, and I'm deep in notes. Dave's at work right now, definitely moving an afternoon bowel, typing away in our "notes" on his phone. Good for him! That's actually where the Craigslist ad was born, in a stall over at Discovery Channel on the seventh floor. If he wasn't going to get fired before, that disclosure should be the nail in the coffin. Sorry, Dave. You were poop-grunting while being creative—that's multitasking. You're a real company man; they'd be foolish to let you go. Anyway, this past summer, Dave and I were hitting "notes" pretty hard.

Every time you opened up "Stangle Notes," you read the last person's disgusting and disturbed thoughts, experiences, and ideas. We had a lot of them, too. It was a strange time. Stangle Notes became our drawing board, message board, and *Real World*–style drunk confession room. After you finish reading this chapter, think about finding someone to share a notes folder with. You two will learn so much about each other!

I was thumbing through Stangle Notes recently and came across a pretty strange, pretty disturbing entry. And that's saying something. This entry really struck a nerve. I honest to God hadn't remembered writing it. . . . I didn't even really remember the night it was *written,* until I checked the date of the entry and reread the post a few times.

After reading this entry, I tried six different times to figure out how to put it in context for you. But you know what? I give up! I shouldn't have to sit here and struggle to make Dave sound normal. He isn't; he's a freak who is really good at coming off as normal to most people most of the time. I emailed Dave a copy of what I reread in the notes and told him I was having trouble writing the piece and thought a thorough Q&A might jolt my memory. Then it occurred to me—did Dave even remember this? I dove in headfirst with the Q's, and couldn't believe how well he remembered the A's. What follows is our attempt to put together the pieces.

Mike: Let's get the facts straight here, Dave. July 13, 2013. Brant Lake, the Great Adirondacks. Nature everywhere. Just how long had it been since you'd last been . . . romantic?

Dave: About forty-five minutes, maybe an hour.

Mike: No, not with yourself.

Dave: Oh weeks. Three, maybe even a month. I know that a month isn't really that long, but it was the summer. There were gals in 'kinis everywhere I looked. And it was hot. People all around me were having sex with one another at an alarming pace. Everyone but me. So it was a long month. If a meteorologist had assessed the situation at the time, he would have given it a "real feel" of seven to nine weeks.

Mike: That has always been your biggest flaw. When you get backed up, you go crazy and become a deviant. I've never seen horniness create such a Dr. Jekyll and Mr. Hyde transformation over someone like it does to you. It's like the minute after you sleep with someone, you're the best guy going, then every additional day that goes by, your thoughts get darker and more fucked-up. Does Brant Lake bring back nostalgic feelings of high school 'gasms?

Dave: I would compare getting funky up at Brant Lake to getting funky in a nice hotel room. Hotel sex is crazy. It's on a different level than normal sex. You can't compare it. Is melted cheese the same thing as regular cheese? No. Add that one word—*melted*—and everything changes. Add *hotel* or *Brant Lake* in front of *sex* and you've got a different animal on your hands. That sort of environment is the last place a dangerously horny twenty-eight-year-old fella needed to be. Everywhere I looked, every step I took, all I saw was places around the campgrounds where I used to finger my high school girlfriend.

Mike: Set the scene up for us. You and I had just come off a pretty wild few days in Nantucket acting like frat boys, if I recall. Did we go straight from there to Brant Lake? Paint me a picture here.

Dave: We got up to camp after a really swell island bender in Nantucket, during which you were constantly surrounded by women while playing the "local cool guy" shtick. Meanwhile, across the bar, I couldn't form coherent sentences and accidently called this cute Asian chick an "Oriental." I couldn't have been striking out more. I think my pants were too tight. The gals didn't pick up what I was putting down. Camp seemed like the best place to be next, so we headed there for relaxation. We greeted our folks, a couple relatives, Denny poured us some bucket-sized glasses of wine, and we watched the dogs run around and play. They even humped a little bit. I knew things weren't right when even that revved my engine. It was great to be back at camp, enjoying good company and cheap wine, taking a cruise on *The Entertainer*. The next several hours and several days rolled on, as they always did, year in and year out. Family time, the *Forrest Gump* sound track blasting at all times, lawn games, really huge and over-the-top meals, cocktails to match those meals, laughs for days, JT starting massive fires the second the sun set every night. We were getting mileage out of *The Entertainer* like you wouldn't believe that year. After twenty-five years of service, he had just been reupholstered and was looking mighty fine. It was like that boat was just always welcoming us with open arms and stocked coolers. *Come on board, fellas, have a few drinks on me. Literally on me. I'm a boat.*

Mike: Whoa, whoa, whoa. Rewind. I've got to give some background here. We didn't do *any* of that until we headed next door to greet the neighbor, Jim. Jim is crazy. He should be crazy, by all means; he is ninety-four years old. He has lived next door to the lake house forever. The guy has the most insane crush on our mother that any man has had on any woman. It would be over the line if he wasn't so darn cute and bashful. Plus, can you blame him? Denny has been a babe for decades now. She's like a lady Pierce Brosnan. Now, to be clear—Jim is 100 percent senile. Our entire family has watched it slowly develop over the last five or six years. Every summer we get up here, he has one foot just a little further off the merry-go-round. Alzheimer's, dementia, flatulence, you name it. It was sad. My dad will claim Jim has been crazy for years, but I'm certain that before all of that health stuff really started affecting him, he just pretended it was way worse than it was. Why? So he could be all handsy with Denny and not have to answer for it. What a sick pup! I've got to respect that move, though. What old-man balls of steel he had. One time, he actually brought a package of men's tighty-whitey underwear over as a "welcome back to camp" gift to my mom. Hanes eight-pack, XL. Well played, Jim.

Mike: Anyway, we know you were lonely and horny that night . . . but just *how* horny and lonely?

Dave: Lonely and horny are like two dangerous drugs you should never mix together. They are a lethal combo. The difference is that with drugs, you can choose to do just one or the other and keep things under control. You can't control how horny or how lonely you are, so when they both come at you at the same time, you're totally fucked. You know when it's coming, too. You can hear Egon from *Ghostbusters* in your head yelling "Don't cross the streams!!!" It's the perfect storm of male vulnerability, and there is simply nothing you can do about it except hope you come out on the other end without making too many regrettable decisions. Oh, and that never happens.

Mike: When your streams did finally cross, what made the Stay Puft Marshmallow Man come marching down Central Park West?

Dave: It was the booze. It wasn't like pouring gasoline on a campfire; it was like pouring jet fuel on the Springfield Tire Fire. The more I drank to suppress my emotions (always a solid plan), the worse it got. The more bourbon that went down the hatch, the more ballsy I got with my texts, the more two-plus-year-old Instagram photos of exes I liked, the more deep sighs I took. By dinnertime, I couldn't even eat. I remember thinking, *No. No ribs for you. Ribs are for closers.* It was code red. A thousand. A thousand what? No idea. Just a thousand. I was texting every girl I've ever known. I was texting gals I didn't even know. I texted a random number saved in my phone as "BIG OL' GOOD GIRL." I have no clue who it was, when I put it in my phone, or why I decided those were the best four words to describe someone whose number I was obtaining. Naturally, I gave her the late-night classic "You up?" No response. I tried to text contacts in my phone that were so old that they were landlines. Remember dealing with those? *Hi, this is Dave, how are you? Great, thanks for asking! Say, is Jenny around?* The only text I sent that night that didn't originate directly from my penis was the text to lawyer and good ol' boy Nick Braman. I wanted to make sure my retainer was fully paid and my affairs were in order. The only words I could get out to him were "Buckle Up." By now, he knows what that means.

Mike: So . . . you texted every gal in your phone and the fish that ended up on the hook was the bisexual architect? How did you even know her?

Dave: Well, technically, I didn't know her. I had never met her before that night. Ever. Remember during the Craigslist fiasco when we were getting more attention from females than two guys have ever deserved in the history of Earth? Back then there were so many emails, Facebook requests, and AOL IMs (yup, still use it) we couldn't keep things straight, so we resorted to text. Huge mistake. Talk about getting streams crossed. I was texting with all of these random numbers all the time, not knowing who was who or what was going on. I was just going with it and seeing what happened. Months later, the gals who were wise lost interest, but a few stuck around.

Mike: As I remember it, she agreed to drive the hour and a half from the Albany area up to Brant Lake after you dropped her a pin of where we were on Google Maps. It's pitch black out, there was a full moon (never helpful when horny), and she arrived at the stroke of midnight. The entire time she had been driving up, we had been working our way through our Montana Coolers [if you don't know what that is, google "Bill Murray Montana Cooler"]. When she arrived, we made an alarmingly small amount of small talk before settin' sail on *The Entertainer* for a late-night booze cruise. She wasn't the slightest bit uncomfortable. Not the *least* bit weirded out by the circumstances. There was funny business brewing from the start, and we needed to get offshore. That is my last lucid memory of the night. After that, the Montana Coolers were basically in charge.

Dave: Weren't you driving *The Entertainer*?! Was it driving itself? Where was I?

Mike: Fuck you, man. Yes I was driving, but it didn't really count as *drunk* driving, because we were on a boat that couldn't exceed fifteen miles per hour. Anyway, I didn't have the luxury of a bisexual architect with librarian glasses sitting in my lap. With a full moon casting ample light on the whole scene. See what I'm getting at?

Dave: Things did start out innocent enough. We smoked some of that funny grass you like; BA [bisexual architect] and I slowly got into some cupcakin' and honey-holdin' as the jam box was playing all the right tunes.

Mike: It's time to tell us about the '9ing playlist. You owe it to us.

Dave: All I'll say is that over the course of

several months, I might have crafted the perfect private playlist on Spotify, titled *'9ing,* and it might do an incredibly effective job of getting the natural pheromones of anyone listening on the same page.

Mike: I want that playlist, Dave.

Dave: One day, when it is published, it will be my greatest contribution to mankind. The world doesn't need that kind of heat right now.

Mike: As we were floating in the middle of the lake, you two started smooching pretty hard. I know you're not a big PDA guy, and I can understand you letting your guard down when the only P watching the DA is me, but you were really going at it. I was surprised. Soon that surprise turned to disgust, then it turned to alarm. I couldn't believe what I was watching develop. I knew you were horny, but I didn't know it was to the level of what I was watching.

Dave: It became one of those "I'll stop if you stop" scenarios with her, and you know neither one of us ever comes out on the right end of those. It felt so good to touch someone, especially someone who was as able to ignore your presence as I was. When she took her shirt off, I thought, This is happening! Do you remember what you yelled aloud when she did that?

Mike: "Holy mackerel!"

Dave: It didn't matter that you were screaming phrases our parents used so they wouldn't take the Lord's name in vain; the heat was on when that shirt came off. I will say that there were parts of me that felt weird about it with you right there. I was barreling toward a stop sign I knew I'd blow through, though. I did, very briefly, think about how strange this was about to become for you.

Mike: No, you didn't. The only considerate thing you did was position her naked body in between us, so I at least didn't have to see your nudity.

Dave: You're welcome.

Mike: At that point, I still thought she was just going to get naked, and I was telling myself that was it, and this would be a pleasant treat for the both of us. When did it turn the corner?

Dave: This entire experience was so blurry, but the one lucid memory I do have was this: I was wearing these highlighter yellow shorts with an elastic waist. She pulled the waistline out away from my stomach and looked down, then looked back up at me as if she was saying "For meee?" I don't know what made me say what I said next, but out it came: "Go for it." You know what was funny? When her head and torso bent down at a ninety-degree angle toward my wiener, all of a sudden you and I were staring at each other! That was some awkward eye contact, huh? I didn't know where else to look!

Mike: Gross! I'm having flashbacks. It's burned into my skull. I can't believe at one point I was thinking about trying to steal her from you. Or weirder, maybe try to join in, just to see how much crazier it could get? I don't know! We were in the middle of a lake, man. All sorts of stuff goes through a guy's head.

Dave: Had I known then what I know now about BA, I'd have put my money on that happening with little to no resistance.

Mike: I wouldn't have had the chance, anyway. You lasted what . . . ten seconds?

Dave: Real feel? Twelve seconds.

Mike: And I thought you stopped because you came to your senses when you remembered how strange it is to hump a total stranger in front of your younger brother in the middle of a lake. Had I known you stopped because you were finished, I would have made fun of you way harder.

Actual Live Notes

I just watched you have sex. For like ten seconds. Were you done? What WAS that? Then after, I am pretty confident she was about to literally move on to me, but your cupcakin' bonds were too strong. I probably had 6 drinks just now on the boat because I didn't know what else to do. This stinks! I don't know whether to write about it so I don't forget, or just actually try and forget that I watched you give that gal a pussy job. Shit. I feel like we've crossed a line (BECAUSE OF YOU) that we just can't turn back from. I'm calling it quits on our partnership/brotherhood.

"Mike, can we fuck in front of you if she gets naked and blocks my body and penis?"

This is ridiculous. I'm captain of the fucking love boat

*and you're over there taking advantage of your unde-
feated "9ing" playlist. You're finger-banging a bisexual
architect in librarian glasses, while I stare at you guys and
lament out loud about how horny/disgusted I am—she's
even sympathizing with me! I bet I could bang her during/
after you. Ugh, gross. I just poured the strongest drink of
all time. There's no turning back from this, Dave.*

Molly. Roofalin?

(Dave)

I just woke up. It's 11 something a.m. on a Saturday. It's the fall of 2012 in New York City. I'm immediately overcome with one of the few feelings I both hate and am consistently unable to avoid: waking up and having no idea what the FUCK happened the night prior, combined with not being able to find my phone to piece it together. The longer I have to wait for the forensics, the worse I assume I behaved. It happens here and there with me, mostly when I drink too much. Actually it only happens when I drink too much, but this time I mean I didn't remember drinking that much at all. I also usually have a pretty reliable drunk fail-safe. The damage is never that bad, because once I get to that level, I pretty much have twenty minutes of being a raving lunatic, then go directly to bed in a compromising position. It's like clockwork. Once in a while, I'll grope a buddy's girlfriend or puke somewhere public. But usually the feedback is along the lines of "Oh, you weren't too bad. You were real fucked-up, yup, but didn't do anything too bad." Still, I have to be able to assess the potential of the previous night's missteps by analyzing the forensics, and I can't do that without my phone. I can't find it anywhere, and I start to freak out. I barely trust myself when I'm sober.

My mind was racing as I realized how little I actually remembered. In fact, I didn't remember *any*thing. Why were things so foggy? Put it together, Dave. I had to actually turn on the TV to see what time it was, since I couldn't find my phone. Okay, let's see, 11 something a.m. on a Saturday in the fall of 2012 in New York. That means I had a Button Hooker[1] flag football game in less than an hour. I decided to do a full sweep of the apartment for my phone before heading out for the game. As I declared my shoe-box-sized bedroom "clear" (aloud, like a SWAT team leader), I moved into the living room. I immediately noticed some weird colored shit on the floor. As I explored the apartment looking for my phone, all I could see was more weird colored shit. It was everywhere. Everywhere! I gave my eyes thirty seconds to focus and began investigating. Once I found my glasses, I picked some of it up and held it closer for examination. They were feathers. Very distinct feathers. Peacock feathers. It looked like someone ran over the NBC peacock with a lawn mower, in my living room. My first

---

1   The Button Hookers were a coed two-hand touch football team my friend Tim ran for the better part of a dozen seasons in NYC. We were quite possibly the most unathletic and unsuccessful franchise in league history. I was arguably *the* most unathletic player on the Button Hookers, despite appearing brawny and active as well as having a larger wingspan than almost anyone in the entire league. After 6 seasons on the Button Hookers I retired with 4 total receptions, 0 touchdowns, 0 interceptions, 24 dropped passes, and 7 ejections by the referee (one of whom was a good friend of mine).

thought was that Matt Lauer was somehow involved as revenge for all those selfies we took on his phone. Then I remembered Matt Lauer is a sweetheart and revenge isn't his game. My next thought was a bit more rational: was it part of a costume? They really didn't feel fake, though. If this was part of a costume, it was very high-end. You cannot imagine my confusion at this point. I picked one up. Fucking huge. I thought maybe, just maybe, I ended up at some sort of *Eyes Wide Shut*–type party where everyone was fucking each other while wearing masks? And maybe I met a gal in a peacock mask and we did a bunch of freaky stuff, so the feathers went flying everywhere? After realizing how ridiculous this sounded as my first assumption, I started doing some real investigating. I smelled the feather. Gamey. Son of a bitch, I don't have time for this. And where is my iPhone? I can only answer all your questions the same way I answered them myself at the time: *in the most confusing manner possible*.

11:40 a.m.: Hungover, confused, and curious, I managed to pull myself together, put on my Button Hooker gold jersey (I lost my original jersey, so I now rock a yellow T-shirt I found at No Relation Vintage in the East Village; it has a Rastafarian guy on it who says, "Jamaican Me Crazy!" It's so on point), and rush out the door with Frank in tow. Frank is the team mascot for the Button Hookers, which is ironic because he isn't physically capable of running an actual button-hook pattern and he *hates* footballs. He steals every single one he can and then destroys it. What a shitty mascot. Frank and I got to the field within ten minutes of game time. Fellow Button Hookers rejoiced. I felt good, like they were genuinely happy I was there. My teammates on the Button Hookers are also my best friends. I tried asking everyone about what had happened the night before, but everyone gave me that look that said *you know what you did*. Are you guys being ironic? I don't know what I did. Honestly!

12 p.m.–1 p.m.: Game time. I wasn't feeling so hot. I had the spins, then took a personal time-out for a quick sideline spit-up. You know those spit-ups when you aren't quite throwing up, but your body is still telling you something has to come out? I had those for a while, then I drank all of my water, then all of my teammates' water, then I stole some from our ref. I was hurting. At halftime, I started fishing for clues from my friends. Steve immediately informed me that he could not believe I was still breathing and that he had already been writing my obituary. Okay. Good start. Apparently, attempts at reaching me all morning proved futile, and he had been telling anyone who would listen that I was dead. The last time he saw me was at 11 p.m. He could only say I

was drinking "like you had a bone to pick." And he left me shortly thereafter. Tim didn't provide much more insight. He walked by me, looked me in the eye, threw his head back with one stiff laugh, slapped me *really* hard on the back, and kept on walking. That's all he could offer.

The game ended, and I forcefully corralled the gang. It was at this point that the guys finally filled me in about my night from their perspective. Apparently, around midnight I had met a nice gal and we seemed to hit it off. I do remember that part. For well over an hour, this gal proceeded to very publicly seduce me (their words, not mine). I remember that, too. She was like a snake charmer! She played her little flute and out peeked its head from the basket, ready to dance for her. I was told that she and I had a very public make-out and that I wouldn't stop telling anyone who would listen that I was "smitten." I don't quite remember that part. Sometime shortly after, she asked me to taste some of the molly she had hidden deep within her bosom. I was helpless. Fucking snake charmer, you guys. My friends were also careful to note two things:

1. That the molly she was offering (seducing me with, really) didn't look like any molly they'd ever seen before.

2. That I did not care *whatsoever* what she was giving me, I was in. They said she put a few of these little chunks of stuff in my hand and I popped them into my mouth as I asked, "What are these things? *Do you want to dance?*"

1:30–2 p.m.: The walk home with Frank was rough. I had to clear my head and figure out what happened. I stopped to get some froyo, which helped as always.

What the fuck did this girl feed me? Also, did she have a live peacock in her pocketbook? Was it some sort of sexy costume? *Where the fuck* is my phone? I need that! Dammit. All I could pull together was that I ate some weird substance that was most likely not the substance I was told it was, and BOOM, lights out. Roofies? Do they actually exist? What the hell? Back at my apartment, I did some research. As I got comfortable among the peacock feathers, I fired up the Google machine. Let's get to the bottom of this.

2:30– . . . All right, that's it—I will find out what's going on here, and I don't care how much it costs me. After some consideration and a weird amount of pot, I decided it was time for results. Hello, Emergency Room. How long could this take, anyway?

9–10:30—Clearly the good people of Beth Is-
rael Medical Center did not deem my medical
emergency an actual "medical emergency."
I'm not saying that my situation should have
taken priority over some of the gore you see in
a New York City ER, but I was so hungover that
I at least *looked* like I needed emergency attention. That was what convinced me to go to the
ER in the first place. I'll put nearly anything in
my body, but I've got to know what it is. It took
so long, that ER visit. I shouldn't have written
down on the form that I was visiting the ER
because I believe I was roofied and a peacock
stole my iPhone. Six and a half hours later, I got
to see the friendly little Asian doctor. I twisted
my story around a bit to make it seem like more
of a medical emergency with real-world conse-
quences, rather than my quest to find out who
or what was in my apartment the night before
and maybe, upon answering that question,
find out where the hell my phone was. This guy
straight up did not believe me. But if at first
you don't succeed, make up more shit until you
get your way. Dr. Woo finally (reluctantly) took
some tests. The toxicology report? Roofalin.
The peacock spiked my punch. Well, that explains the complete black hole in the space my
memories used to occupy. Next step, peacock
feathers.

Two to three weeks later: After the toxicology report came back, my friends never let me hear the end of it. They couldn't believe a girl seduced me, then roofied me. And no one could let the peacock feathers go. Soon my friend Howard suggested I send them to a lab downtown to find out if they were real. It would cost $499, and he convinced every single person on our email chain to kick in a portion. I had a deep moment of introspection when I sent off a check for $499 and an envelope of feathers in order to determine if I was robbed by a bird. In the meantime, I replaced my iPhone. This was my seventh iPhone of 2012. By the way, did you know that the iPhone insurance people stop insuring you after your sixth iPhone? I am iPhone uninsurable. They said I had to go at least eight months without losing or breaking one before I could reapply for coverage. What bullshit.

It was a Monday when the email came through and I gathered up a few friends on speakerphone to hear the results. The lab tech was very formal in informing me that the feathers in question had been analyzed. She proceeded to explain that before she could say any more, I'd have to contact the NYPD directly with a reference number she gave me. Okay. Uh, *what*?

Naturally I hung up the phone immediately, told my friends to leave, lowered the blinds, and locked the door. I closed the book on the whole shebang right then and there. Wouldn't you? I'm not bringing the NYPD into this! I walked away and took a very important lesson with me: Don't take pills if you don't know what they are. Even if a pretty girl plucks them from her bosom. Especially then. Were you looking for a neat ending to this story, perhaps an odd but ultimately satisfactory answer to the peacock mystery? So was I! But this is what happens when you do drugs.

(Too Much) Grass

(Dave)

Sometimes when you eat too much of ordinary foods with extraordinary ingredients, shit gets a little animated. I would never recommend getting to this Toon Town level of high. Grass is so fun, but it's for relaxing, not for hallucinating. The last time I got to animation-level high was with Mike, naturally. Mike and I had a big weekend planned. It was Memorial Day, so we wanted to make some memories. Being the upstate freshwater guys we are, we rented an island on Lake George. An entire island! The parks commission in Lake George rents out individual sites on all the islands on Lake George, but they didn't foresee two psychopaths renting out every available site on one island so they could be lunatics without being disturbed. We had a real motley crew on board for Stangle Island, too. Quack, Frank the Dog, Nick Waldrip from the South, Slime Dog, you name it. And of course, not a single female in sight. Would *you*, as a woman, go to an island alone with that crew? Me neither.

The problem with this particular Memorial Day weekend was that the forecast was basically calling for a monsoon. You can tell shit is going to hit the fan when all the meteorologists have their jackets and ties off, sleeves rolled up. Al Roker told everyone a monsoon was coming, so everyone bailed. Everyone but Mike and me. And Frank. Oh and Slime Dog, too. Slime Dog never bails. We were determined to party on Dave Island, despite the ensuing monsoon. In the absolutely sideways rain, the three of us drove up to Lake George in the middle of the night, launched *The Entertainer* in the pitch black, and set out for Stangle Island. We made it about thirty-five feet into the bay before bailing. What the *fuck* were we thinking? No, literally, that was what the cop asked us when we were struggling to get *The Entertainer* back on the trailer in 60 mph winds. We got it on, though, then we ditched it in the parking lot of the Howard Johnson's we'd be staying in for the night. As we were ditching *The Entertainer* in the parking lot, a large black woman standing in the lobby didn't seem to care at all. We came in from the wilderness, creatures void of form. "Come in," she said. "I'll give ya shelter from the storm." So we went in.

Inside our luxurious HoJo room, we immediately took inventory of our supplies. We had four handles of bottom-shelf bourbon, three liters of ginger ale (diet, obviously), access to an ice machine, 6 gummy bears dipped in acid (for a special occasion), well over an ounce of grass, 3 cigarillos, 5 Ambien, 0 dry clothes, 6 pot brownies whose seller claimed they would "put down a pregnant rhino," and Frank the Bulldog. We decided that after such a long night, we should have some "feel-good" time. For the next several hours, the scene in that HoJo room remained relatively constant. While their wet clothes hung in the bathroom, three grown males wearing nothing but hand towels crushed down Shitty Daves (ice, heavy pour of bourbon, splash of diet ginger, a little poured out for dead homies) like it was some sort of competition. We wanted some grass, but had too much respect for Mr. HoJo to smoke in his room. Wait a tick, we don't need to smoke! Edibles, here we come! On top of those, at around 11:30 p.m. we each took an Ambien, figuring they would knock us out until the storm had passed. Then we really ran into trouble. *Who Framed Roger Rabbit* came on HBO Kids ('cause you know HoJo has the baller cable package) and we had no choice but to fight the drug, so we could stay up to watch it. Have *you* ever fought off Ambien successfully? When combined with a *ton* of grass and booze? Welcome to Toon Town, my friends. An hour and a half later, we were on the moon, and we weren't going to waste such a unique buzz wasting away in a HoJo while there was an entire world out there just waiting to be frightened by our general appearance. We put on our wet clothes, and Frank the Bulldog insisted on driving us into town. He executed a textbook parallel park on the strip, and we walked toward the bar scene.

Christie's On The Water. CLOSED. King Neptune's. CLOSED. Legends Bar & Grill. CLOSED. Moose Tooth Grill. NO DOGS ALLOWED. The Boat House. LIFETIME BAN. We were striking out left and right. Defeated, we took shelter under the awning of what we thought was a closed and possibly haunted gift shop. As we puffed away at a one-hitter (because someone decided we weren't high enough yet?) the door swung open and the sweet sound of AC/DC poured out into the street. The haunted gift shop wasn't a haunted gift shop at all, but an actual bar—a secret bar for the locals, called Judd's Tavern. Considering we looked like we just escaped from a mental institution, we looked *exactly* like Lake George locals. Naturally, we went inside and carved out a spot. We sat in a triangle at a booth, all facing in toward one another, as Frank settled in underneath for a nap. It was 3 a.m., after all, plus, all he does is sleep. We had also put this tiny little rain jacket and Hawaiian shirt on him. They weren't dog clothes; they were for a kid. We know this because some family with a roomful of kids next to ours had hung them out to dry. Don't you know you're supposed to hang clothes to dry in the bathroom, or else they are fair game?

It was a good thing Frank was looking sharp, because Judd's Tavern wasn't the friendliest scene. It seemed like everyone was giving us the stink eye. At first I thought it must have been in our heads, paranoia due to the wild mixture of chemicals in our blood. Still, we minded our own business. Two nights earlier, Mike had enjoyed a wild drunken night, during which an old flame located and tracked him down and brought him home for a slumber party. As he tells it, she stripped from the waist up and fell asleep on top of him. Not like in a sexy kind of on top of him, but more like the passed-out-cold on top of him. She then began peeing in her sleep. He tried to roll her off him when he felt the pee, but he became trapped between her sleeping body and the wall. He proceeded to use her body as a gymnastics-style vaulting horse and executed a textbook front handspring away to safety. That safety proved only momentary, as Mike's acrobatics had awoken the beast. She came to consciousness in a drunken rage and started chasing Mike, pee pants and all.

Trapped, confused, and scared, he did the only thing that made sense to him at the time. He grabbed his iPhone and snapped several pictures as he was running away, trying to escape from her. The pictures were absolutely priceless. A drunk, drooling topless chick with pee all over her white jeans (it was before Labor Day) chasing Mike from her lair. Mike's POV photo sequence made her look remarkably like what I can only describe as a really hot, angry zombie. Arms out, the weird stagger. Everything. Every time he swiped to the next photo in the twenty-plus sequence he took, we laughed harder and harder. Mike would pull up a picture, burst out laughing, then explain what was happening in it before he held it up for Slime Dog to look, then me. It was a sequence that got funnier each time. After about fifteen minutes of what I can only describe as hyena-type laughter every time we were shown a photo, our table was approached by a couple of local girlies. Actually they weren't girlies at all; they were full-blown women. *Local* women. The lead woman, well, she was a real bitch. There was no "hello," no "y'all from 'round here?," no "why do you have a dog in the bar?" Instantly, right away, the first thing she did was grab at Mike's phone and demand to know why we were taking pictures of her and her friends. Her friends stood behind her, confident and pissed-off, with their hands on their hips. Having no idea where she was coming from, we simply told her the truth. We weren't taking pictures of her at all. We hadn't even noticed her, or her friends. Slime Dog went so far as to tell her he wouldn't have noticed her if he walked by her in a desolate western town. That probably wasn't the right thing to say. Soon we were in a full-blown argument. The lead bitch thought we were taking pictures of her and laughing at them as we passed Mike's iPhone around the table. We assured her that wasn't the case. It didn't matter. We were in a pickle: of course we weren't taking pictures of this woman and her friends. But could we prove it? We were *not* about to show her the pictures we'd actually been looking at. She'd freak! Phone exchanges were being demanded, tensions were high, Frank was barking.

This is where the strength of edibles really shows its muscle. You know you're not on a hard drug, so you're not hallucinating, but the things happening around you are too absurd to be real. Within thirty seconds, Judd's Tavern turned into the set of *Judge Judy*. Our party was gathered up on one side of the bar, Bitch Lady and her cronies were around the corner on the other side of the bar, and Judge Judd—the owner of the tavern—was presiding over the case. Everyone else in the bar had gathered around us. They either sat behind Slime Dog, Frank, Mike, and me or they sat behind the bitches. It was a pretty even split. The bitches started with their opening statement. It focused mostly around us being "city creeps" and "perverts" who came into a local establishment uninvited and clearly on drugs. Pretty spot-on, so far. I found it odd that she didn't at all address the fact that we had a dog in the bar, dressed in human clothing.

She presented a strong case, and Judd, ever so wise in the ways of a barroom dispute, nodded his head in approval. We were in for an uphill battle, or so I thought, until Mike got up for his turn. I'm not sure why Mike was designated as our team leader, but now that I know what kind of performance he was about to deliver, I'm sure glad he was. It was magical. It was like he was preparing for this trial his entire life. He was like McConaughey in *A Time to Kill* combined with McConaughey from *The Lincoln Lawyer*. It was as if for his entire life he had defended his right to keep nude pictures of peeing women chasing him, and this was just a walk in the park. He tucked in his shirt. He spoke slowly and with a southern drawl. He asked the Honorable Judge Judd and the local jurors rhetorical questions that swayed them toward our side. I couldn't believe what I was seeing. How high was I? Was Mike suddenly and out of nowhere wearing a white suit? Where did he get that Bible he had clasped under his arm, as he slowly paced back and forth in front of Judd? Where did he learn to use words like *acquiesce* and *repudiate*? He was fucking brilliant. When he was done, Slime Dog, Frank, and I all stood up and erupted in applause. Slime Dog was crying. I couldn't believe the rest of the bar didn't join us.

By the time Mike "rested his case," Judd had heard enough. He was ready to deliver his verdict. We all exchanged looks like people do right before they are about to receive an award. There were pats on the back all around. Judd started by stating that absolutely nothing Mike said made any sense at all, to anyone, and that Mike was to be immediately cut off from the bar for the rest of the night, although Slime Dog and I were welcome to finish our drinks so long as we behaved. Mike screamed "Objection!" right away, but Judd said he wasn't finished. He turned to Patty-Anne (*of course* that was her name) and gave her a verbal lambasting like I've never heard. He told her he was sick of her shit, and no one in their right mind would ever take a picture of her because it would break their phone. One of his goons escorted Patty-Anne and her friends out as she gave us the double middle finger over her shoulder. The bar became quiet. Slime Dog sheepishly looked up at Judd and asked, "Did we . . . win?" His reply: What the *hell* are you guys on?

Dave clearly got into something this night. One-piece pajamas? Feet seem to be tar-and-feathered. Great butt, though.

Goofballs

(Mike)

I don't know why we got to calling them "goofballs" instead of "hallucinogenic mushrooms," but we did. And sometimes when you eat a coupla goofballs, shit gets weird. Dave and I eat goofballs once a year. It's refreshing to get outside your own mind once in a while. What would become a Stangle boy tradition had its start one summer when I was living in Nantucket. It began with a simple "Want some?" and in response, "Sure." What followed were eight of the most reflective, blissful, giggly, silly, confusing, clarifying hours either of us had in years. We started taking one day a year to get the fuck outta Dodge, bury reality, eat some goofballs, and just see what happens.

The first inaugural goofball weekend was actually completely unplanned. Dave visited while I was living out my white-guy college fantasy on Nantucket. Do you guys know how magical a place Nantucket is? It isn't just the WASPy fantasy land for rich folks that its reputation suggests. Sure, there are rich white folks there, but there are rich white folks pretty much everywhere these days, except Compton. Located thirty miles due south of Cape Cod, Massachusetts, Nantucket is a quaint island first

populated by the Wampanoag people. Its native inhabit-
ants, the Wampanoags, lived undisturbed until as late as
1641, when white guys came in and fucked shit up. Also,
in the 1970s, Nantucket (along with neighboring babe
island Martha's Vineyard) unsuccessfully attempted to
secede from the commonwealth of Massachusetts. So
you know they're badass.

Ever since, it's been a haven for white collars and
high brows. Nantucket itself is an incredible place.
Beaches and views and wildlife and foliage and sunsets
and pretty girls and all that shit. The problem is that all
that stuff is pretty much *too* awesome. People want it.
And then people start to pay money for it. Then more
money! The first time I ever went there, everyone was
named Griff McKallister or Caulfield Waylensby. Those
names spit on a name like Mike Stangle. I actually tried
to shine one guy's shoes, totally out of instinct. What
the hell was that about? Those guys weren't around
the weekend in question, though. It was just me, Dave,
Frank the Bulldog, our buddy Steveo, and a shitload
of mushrooms. Oh, and Dave's jam box! That thing is
clutch.

Steve had never eaten mushrooms before and was
scared shitless of them. Months earlier in New York, we
got Steve to agree to try them if he ever fell under what
he considered to be unlikely circumstances. *Oh sure,
guys, I'll take mushrooms—if I'm ever with you and Mike
on a deserted island and we somehow find mushrooms,
that's when I'll eat them. But you BOTH have to be there.*

Oh yeah, and Frank has to be there. And it has to be Au-
gust. And we can't plan it.

Well, wouldn't ya know it, I was living on an island
in August. Dave had planned a trip out to visit and naturally brought Frank the Bulldog with him, because Frank
loves white girls and islands. Oh, what's that, Steve? You
have a wedding to go to on Cape Cod and you've got a
few days to kill, because you want to avoid your future
in-laws as much as possible? No problem, hop on the
ferry, pal.

When this scenario started to play out, Dave and I
were immediately on the same page before either of us
had said a word. All he did was look at me in a very specific way, and I promptly pulled out the mushrooms that
a stranger had handed to me a few nights prior. Sounds
legit, right? It was a Tuesday. I worked the day shift while
Steve and Dave spent the day with Frank on the beach.
Dave and I had this whole secret plan that involved
mushroom-and-peanut-butter sandwiches. Steve loves
PB sandwiches; he can't resist them! We figured it'd be
the path of least resistance. We also have him on video
agreeing to the "ridiculous" terms of his mushroom
proposal, which Dave had cued up in case he put up any
sort of fight. The guys spent the *entire* day at the beach,
and Dave didn't even so much as hint anything to Steve.
That's self-discipline if I've ever heard of it. Nice work,
Dave. I finished my day shift around four, walked out
of my restaurant, and immediately hopped into my old
Wrangler that Dave was driving. It was so smooth, he

didn't even stop—I just hopped right in while he was roll-ing along the cobblestones. We were in for a good one.

About fifteen minutes later, we arrived at the scene of the crime. A remote beach we could drive out on, far enough away from anyone who might mess with us. Steve had consumed a fair amount of day beers and was too happy riding around on a beach in an old Jeep to ask any questions. We parked and Dave started blast-ing Alice Cooper's "Feeding Time" and was just staring at Steve like a lunatic. I whipped out the sandwiches, handed them around, and filled Steve in. It was like he knew exactly what was going on and didn't give a shit. He didn't miss a beat. Took one peek at the contents of the sandwich, gave us the ol' "here goes nothin'," and bit in.

Since this isn't a story about how goddamn fun mushrooms are, I'll only spend a little bit of time on that. Do you guys know how goddamn fun mushrooms are? For five hours, there were three guys and one bull-dog just laughing our asses off. Didn't think dogs could laugh? On mushrooms, they sure can. For five hours, it felt like being seven years old again, but with less hand-eye coordination and more colors. The waves were enormous that day and at one point, we started playing this game that I was calling "Don't Fight It." This name made sense, because the point of the game was to just keep your head above water, let your body go completely limp, and let the waves do what nature intended: toss your ass around. This might sound dumb, and it definitely was. But we were tripping our titties off, so it automatically became hilarious. I have one vivid memory of being beached for a good ten minutes after a monster wave had taken me up onto the sand. I was busy not fighting it, and in that case it meant lying there on the beach till another big wave came in to take me back out to sea. Frank did *not* like this and was very concerned. He tried to fight 90 percent of the waves that came my way, but his anxiety could not be alleviated. I looked up to see Dave sitting crisscross-applesauce on the beach like a little kid, observing the whole thing. The scene in front of him had him laughing so hard that I watched him literally throw up from laughter. Luckily, the mushrooms had taken hold at that point, so the barfing didn't end his trip.

It eventually got dark on the beach and a little too cold to stay out there. The issue here was that we were definitely still out of our minds and my Jeep wasn't going to drive itself. Oh, wait, I'm on a beach, driving ten miles an hour, and there's no one around that I could hurt? Here we go! I drove down the beach for a little bit to test my sobriety. Good enough. Dave then pointed out an off-road trail I'd never seen before, and we immediately followed it. Ever go off-roading on hallucinogens? It is wild. We didn't go faster than three miles an hour, and we loved every second of it. Mud, fallen trees, puddles, small lakes—you name it, we were driving through it (very slowly). We eventually found our way out of the trail and onto the main road, but not before driving through what I remember to be an actual lake. The road we were let out onto was incredibly dark; no streetlights, just a narrow road on an island, pitch-black. I took a left and started driving. After getting up to the speed limit, I let off the gas and something changed. Every single light on my truck immediately turned off. Oh come on! I looked over at the guys, but it was so dark I couldn't even see them from two feet away. Everyone started freaking out. I immediately slowed down and we tried to figure it out. As I came to a stop, we all calmed down. Okay, let's try this again. I accelerated and boom! Lights back on, we were in business. Dave gave me a *that was weird* type look, and we kept on driving. A minute later, it happened again. Steve started freaking out and throwing his empty daytime beer cans out the back of the truck like we were a sinking ship and he was bailing buckets of water. Not cool, Steve, this island has a really delicate eco-balance. After what I remember to be about twenty minutes of this scenario repeating itself, I had almost crashed more times than I will admit here. Why the fuck wouldn't my lights work? If I had been sober or on pretty much any drug besides mushrooms, I probably would've put the pieces together. The exposed wiring on my old-ass Jeep had clearly gotten wet from the lake we had driven through, and that was affecting my electric. Three idiots on mushrooms? We couldn't even grasp the problem, let alone the solution.

Dumb luck connected a few integral synapses in my brain. When I accelerate . . . the lights turn on. What?

Okay, don't question it, just keep the goddamn lights on so we can get home. I was so excited that I couldn't find any other way to explain my findings to the guys other than to scream out "SPEED! LIKE THE MOVIE!" They knew what I meant immediately. I was Keanu Reeves, Dave was Sandra Bullock, and Steveo was Jeff Daniels (he wishes), and I'm pretty sure Frank was playing the role of Dennis Hopper, evil genius. As far as I was concerned, if we slowed down, the car was going to explode. I drove the final ten miles back to my place while doing my best to a) not hallucinate and b) *keep accelerating*. Do you know how hard it is to do both of those things simultaneously? To continuously accelerate while on mushrooms, driving a four-cylinder Jeep along windy island roads? It's pretty tough. And that's why this was the last time we messed with mushrooms.

Holly Humphrey Holy Hell!

(Mike)

We Stangle boys have a thing for crazy women. Call it a trait, call it a type, call it whatever you want. Me? I call it a curse. It's never brought us anything but trouble, really. We can't help ourselves. All we're ever left with is a more fucked-up psyche and maybe a few good stories, and those stories are heavily outweighed by the trouble. Why couldn't we just like gals like our mom? I guess 'cause there's only one out there. It seems that instead, we go for the direct opposite. Denise is levelheaded, grounded, calm, and stoic. You couldn't describe any of our ex-girlfriends in any of those ways. I'd like to feel bad for myself here, but Dave has it worse than I do, and I have it bad. He is into big-leagues crazy. Dave set the bar. He won't even look at a girl twice unless she has spent a minimum of six months in some sort of asylum. I myself like them a little more grounded. If Dave's number-one fantasy crazy gal is chaining him to his bed, lighting his room on fire, then blowing him over the roar of the flames . . . my number-one fantasy crazy gal is doing the same, but maybe just using candles, you know? It still feels nice. You don't always need arson, Dave. I will give him credit, though. Every once in a while, he somehow makes a case for the crazy gals being the most appealing. Sometimes, I dive right in.

One of those times I was living in Nantucket, working at a bar called the Gazebo.

The Gazebo is like the Ellis Island of Nantucket. Everyone must pass through it to gain access to a better life. Also, multiple people leave it with new last names. Unless you arrive to Nantucket via shipwreck, you have to pass through the Gazebo bar. It attracts anyone and everyone on the island. The crowds there get wild, too. We've got all types. The Gazebo sees high-class people, low-class people, drunks, drugs, cash, credit, black cards, blacks, blacks with black cards, whites with no cards, imitation black cards that aren't black but still have that same badass metal credit card feel, foreign nationals, South Boston tough guys, tribal-tattooed New Jersey people (thanks, Hurricane Sandy), and a *ton* of babes! Some of the best people-watching on the planet takes place at the Gazebo. Those holding the black cards are a class among themselves: sailing people, yachting people, August-only people, trust fund babies, guys named Todd. These people might as well have come to Nantucket on the *Mayflower*. My personal favorite among the "black card" category were the trust fund gals. They typically came with highly volatile emotional issues and massive coke problems. I know, I know—on the surface, both are awesome. A fella who had been on Nantucket Island as long as I had knew the rules with this crowd: look, but don't touch. When you go to the zoo, all the tigers look so beautiful and exotic, but that doesn't mean you should hop the fence and start grabbing ass. Dave? He'd strap steaks to his grundle and dive in hoping to get mauled. Me? I try to keep it in the fairway.

Trust fund gals came and went, and I kept my distance as much as I could. Linsley Truesdale. Madeline Caufield. Paisley Cottonwood. Machaela Billowshire. Have you ever seen a better collection of white-girl names? I feel like if any black people read this book, they are probably laughing their asses off for the first and only time right now. Among these trust fund gals was their queen bee—Holly Humphrey. She was like the Beyoncé of fucked-up white girls. When she sang, everyone danced backup.

Holly Humphrey had been named as though her parents knew full well she would later have problems with booze, drugs, guys, intelligence, not squandering the family fortune, basic math, general survival, and all-around mental health and sanity. You name it—she wasn't good at it. The only thing she could do well was be incredibly hot. Holly Humphrey was an absolute 10. She was one of those gals who are very tall and skinny, yet somehow have HUGE natural boobs. She was very fit, too. Her boobs and hair were probably the only soft parts of her body. How does God choose which women He is going to bless with such seemingly unfair natural physical traits? No complaints, I just wish He would make some sort of social network for them, so I could always see what they are up to and where they are checking in.

Holly Humphrey was absolutely bonkers. There isn't a combination of words in the English language to describe how truly crazy this chick is. Had Dave ever met Holly Humphrey, I am 100 percent confident they would have eloped within hours and the two of them wouldn't have surfaced again for over a decade, until their underground lair was discovered deep inside a Thai jungle. The magnitude of her craziness had no boundaries. She was so crazy that you would question your own sanity when talking to her. You'd think, *Wait, what is going on here? There is no way this is real. Have I lost* my *mind?* It inspires some real *Being John Malkovich*–type shit.

I had seen her in the Gazebo multiple times throughout the summer. Before I had ever even met her, I was having a ball simply observing her. I saw the same routine every time she met someone new at my bar. Reading their faces as they reacted to the things she said was so entertaining. First, people were blown away by how attractive she is. Then, before they could get over her beauty, people became confused and disoriented with the things coming out of her mouth. It's like there were four different completely insane people living inside her, and they were all vying for control. It was a goddamn mess.

Holly Humphrey set her eyes on me on the fifteenth of July, 2011. Nantucket Island was at its proverbial full mast. July is when things pick up in a big way on the island. If Nantucket were an eligible bachelor and was making love, and started in early May with some island foreplay, by mid-July, it was rock solid. I mean this island was fuckin' HARD. Babes everywhere, guys wearing tank tops, vanity muscles, badass mopeds, expensive rebuilt retro European SUVs, yachts with celebrities *and* Mini Coopers on board, you get the idea.

So I'm doing my thing, just having a classic "beach kids" type of summer. I'm up to no good, staying up late, getting denied by pretty girls, developing unattractive tan lines, neglecting my physical fitness, and failing to save money. I was like John Cusack in the aptly named *One Crazy Summer*.

So, mid-July. I'm working a lunch shift at the Gazebo. Lunch shifts at the Gazebo are ideal, in that you've only got to work during the day, though they are tough, because 95 percent of the staff is still shitfaced for the start of them. If you could somehow film the staff on a busy day shift, then speed the whole thing up, you could sell it to Discovery Channel as a documentary on alcohol metabolism. At 10 a.m., starting time, all the squares arrive, because they didn't go out the night before. Why are they even living on an island? Ten fifteen to ten thirty rolls around, the booze-smelling (chain smoking, dry-heaving, eyes-as-red-as-the-devil's-dick) portion of the staff shows up. Somehow, the crew comes together and everybody makes a bunch of money. Four fifteen comes along, and I'm still in one piece. As I'm cleaning up behind the bar, I start thinking about which kid's-menu items I'm going to demolish. I look up and *oh,* Holly. Coming by for a cocktail, as I'm finishing my shift. Coincidence? I'd only met her once before this, and she scares the shit out of me—so naturally I clock out, walk to the other side of the bar, and start drinking. Why would I move across the bar and start drinking with a crazy girl who frightens me? It all boils down to the one undeniable fact as old as time itself—men cannot resist beautiful women. Especially one who is into you! I am twenty-one, single, and come aaaahn, she is a babe! Can you blame me? My uncontrollable horniness combines with that weird, what-the-hell-is-happening sort of feeling, and I am all in.

Over the course of the next hour, I consume a healthy four to six bourbons, and Holly Humphrey is not far behind. The girl can drink! Keep in mind we're drinking at the bar I work at, surrounded by my friends and roommates who are all working, and we're being served by my oldest brother's best friend, Alaska. Alaska is from Alaska. Alaska is a giant dickhead and loves fucking with me, especially when it comes to women. Especially when it comes to a crazy woman, and *especially* when he knows just how crazy she is, like this one. As Alaska is overserving us (at four thirty in the afternoon), a revolving crowd is gathering around the bar to listen in on the verbal insanity that is pouring out of Holly's sexy little mouth.

Holly: Alaska, what is your *favorite* gluten-free drink to make?

Alaska: Bud Light.

Holly: *You* don't make that. Mixologists make that before they bottle it. And Bud Light is *not* gluten-free.

Alaska: You're absolutely right.

Holly: But we could google what's in a Bud Light and you could try to make your own version!? Then after, we could just take the gluten out??!

Alaska: I'm going to go now.

Holly: (To me) Is his shift over? He's sweet. Want a Xanax?

Holly Humphrey has a flight to catch. A flight? Today? In an hour? This surprises me. I'm from upstate New York (so sick, you guys) and grew up post-9/11. If I have a flight to catch, I am at the airport with six forms of ID four fucking *months* before that flight, and I'm a white guy! My Arab friends basically have to say the pledge of allegiance just to get car service to take them to the airport. Holly Humphrey has a flight in an hour? I don't get it. Does she have her own crop duster? I thought only farmers had those. I ask her about it, and she pulls this coupon book out of her Birkin bag. It is a complete booklet of airline vouchers. Fifty pages thick, and every single page the same exact thing. A free airline pass. Did you guys know these exist? Did you know they make airline tickets that you just hand to the attendant and then you get on the next flight? I didn't. She has a *book* of those. Holly Humphrey has a flight to catch.

Holly Humphrey's dad is very rich and very angry. He is equally insane, too. Very ill-tempered. It turns out he is also spending some time on the island of Nantucket. Furious, looking for his daughter. I don't know this. All of a sudden, I am made aware. After the twelfth call she has sidebarred (and fourth Stoli O-bomb), I finally ask her who has been calling her. "Just my daddy," she explains. Great. A little more digging, and I put together the obvious. Her father has been calling her because he either:

1. Wants to take her to the airport so she will make her flight.

2. Wants to kill her, because, well . . . I get it.

3. Wants to take her to the airport, so he can have her killed once she's arrived in Boston, giving him an alibi . . . Smart guy, no wonder he's loaded.

Holly Humphrey is ducking calls left and right, looking over her shoulder with fear in her eyes—just trying to avoid her old man. At this point, I've now become drunk enough to be thinking about how badly I'd like to make sweet, crazy, risky, rich-gal love to Holly before her flight. Strategically convenient bonus: my house is right next to the airport! It just made so much sense, everybody. One problem: our only ride is my

'86 Yamaha moped, and I am (as my dad would put it) absolutely cockeyed. Way too drunk to drive. Naturally, I immediately decide to drive. The *real* problem is that my reliable little moped is only 50 cc's (that's an engine term, gals). The thing barely supports my giant, lumbering frame; there is no way it will take on me, Holly, and her five hundred pounds of high-maintenance luggage. I shoot my roommate Tim (also a friend, confidant, state hockey champ, man-babe, and coworker) a glance as he is mixing drinks behind the bar. Tim has seen that glance a thousand times. He no-look throws me his moped keys. Did I mention Tim has a moped, too? We were the Scooter Boys! Good gang name? Nope. But it was very literal. Tim was the leader of the Scooter Boys. You know why? Because Tim has a *sick* moped. The thing absolutely flew. Somewhere along the line, a mechanic did some after-market work on it, and the results made you feel like you were straddling a Tomahawk missile. Added bonus: it was also a two-seater. My '86 Yamaha, although awesome, only had room for one. With me? Just short of room for one. Timmy and I had a gentlemen's understanding that, should either of us be so lucky as to have a gal in tow, the two-seater moped went to that guy. Rules of the road. One might ask what would happen if we were both lucky enough to have a gal on the same night. Well, you've only got one option at that point: expensive group taxi. As luck would have it, we didn't take one group taxi that summer.

Back to reality, folks. I've got a crazy blonde, an

angry rich father, a jacked-up moped, and a race against the clock—let's focus! We find Tim's moped in the back alley of the restaurant. That alley is all cobblestone. Ever ride a moped over three-hundred-year-old New England cobblestone? No? Try it with a ticking-blond-sex-bomb on the back. As we take off down the alley, I am at half-mast before our first RPM. By the time we turn out of the alley, I am at a full tuck-under. With Holly Humphrey on the back and a full erection in my Nantucket reds, we are off! Assuming most of you aren't familiar with the layout of Nantucket, let me fill you in—there is the port, where I work. It's the "downtown" part of the island. The cobblestone alleys bob and weave in every direction, further confirming that *everyone* in New England, even back when the town was being designed, is or was a complete drunk. It's like driving around a child's finger painting. Makes no sense whatsoever. Luckily, the cobblestone keeps people from going too fast; otherwise it'd be accident city. You have to weave through about a cumulative mile of this nonsense to get out of town and on the main roads toward my house, the airport, and intercourse.

Holly Humphrey is holding on tight, and I mean *tight*. I am approaching an intersection about two hundred yards upstream of the Gazebo. I have the right of way, but always look, just to be safe. To my left, BAM, this giant, black, ridiculous, $150,000, tinted-window, red-button-from-MIB-capable, fucking intimidating Mercedes SUV almost splatters my brains and guts and

Holly's tits everywhere. I'm talking within a foot and a half of really doing some damage to us. I swear to God, the SUV coming at us was the Canyonero from *The Simpsons* (12 yards long, 2 lanes wide, 65 tons of American pride!) Do you know how mad Timmy would have been if I wrecked his scooter *and* he had to cover my shifts? True to my BAC, I start yelling at the driver like a madman on a scooter. Just as I'm doing so, Holly Humphrey (on back) buries her head away from the SUV and starts screaming in my ear that that's her dad and to *hit it*! Crazy dad is on to us! Oh, you're wondering if this is the same crazy dad that's been blowing her phone up for the past two hours? Yep. That's him. An angry rich dad looking for his fucked-up daughter who has been avoiding him. The ironic thing is that upon spotting us on the moped, he doesn't get *happier.* I look into his eyes, and he into mine. Had that moment been set in an old western movie, that song would play that always plays right before they say "Draw!" The drawn-out time that two cowboys look each other in the eye is always portrayed as at least fifteen seconds. What were the rules there? *With each cowboy's gun holstered, the two parties are to just stare at each other. At some point, they should have a race to kill the other person. No one will ever say draw. Then one guy dies.* Great plan, Wild West.

Back to reality: Holly's dad is done staring and SHIT IS ON. Holly Humphrey says hit it, so I hit it. We take off down a side street. You know what angry dads do in that kind of situation? They fucking chase you! Thank God

I've had a few drinks, because the chase scene that ensues takes some nerves, my friend. If the Wild West draw song was playing a few seconds before, it has since been replaced by the song that plays during the credits of *The Benny Hill Show.*

It becomes very clear that this town is about to see the David versus Goliath of high-speed chases. Giant Mercedes SUV versus 75 cc moped. Side note here: the speed governor on this particular moped had been removed, because Tim is a badass, so this thing could really fly. Here we are, angry lead-foot dad versus horny half-in-the-bag waiter and real-life Looney Toon on the back. If this were a prizefight, the tale of the tape would favor Angry Daddy by a mile. This is Nantucket, though, my summer homeland. Now, I won't pretend to be well seasoned in the ways of gambling, but I will tell you with confidence that there are three home field advantages a man should never bet against:

1. Tom Brady in Foxboro

2. Justin Timberlake on planet Earth

3. Mike Stangle in Nantucket

I know the town like the back of my dick! Goliath's going down! Off I go, utilizing all 75 cc's of the hog I was riding. LEFT RIGHT SECRET ALLEY LEFT LEFT MORE COBBLESTONES HEY ALEX I'LL SEE YOU TONIGHT AT THE CHICKEN BOX! LEFT RIGHT RIGHT THIS BONER

WON'T GO AWAY! Holly? Oh, she is doing exactly what you'd expect a lunatic of her caliber to be doing: talking dirty/crazy in my ear during the whole fucking thing. That is for the first few minutes. As she realizes I am losing her dad, she further encourages me with an OTPHJ (Outside The Pants Hand Job). Believe it or not, I lose the guy by way of nineteen different side street maneuvers. By the time we sputter into my driveway, Tim's bike is overheating and Holly's finger has fully penetrated my butt.

My friends, I learned something that day. I learned that I am not Dave Stangle. I just can't handle the crazy ones! I'm not built for it. Dave, more for you, buddy. By the time I caught my breath and could digest what had happened over the prior twenty minutes, Holly Humphrey had wandered off to the airport in her high heels. Thank God.

I recently found out Holly was secretly engaged during this entire fiasco. After a little digging, I learned that her fiancé is a big-time coke dealer. Makes sense. I'll probably be murdered for a lousy OTPHJ.

I Farted on a Baby

*And Other Things I Need
to Get off My Chest*

(Dave)

I don't get ashamed easily. It doesn't mean I don't recognize my own flaws; it's just that I'm not trying to improve on them whatsoever. I like being a dirtbag. I own it. Being a dirtbag is only a few shades from being a bad boy, and chicks love bad boys. I'm like a second-rate bad boy, so chicks sort of dig it, but not that much. At least it helps me understand why I'm twenty-nine and still single, with a trajectory path of creepy-forty-six-year-old-uncle-who-people-suspect-might-be-gay-because-he-never-settled-down status. Still, if that's the vibe I give off, then I say most people don't really know me very well. Even my iPhone doesn't know me very well, and I spend most of my time glued to my iPhone. It still autocorrects *butthole* to *buttonhole*, even though I talk about the first thing all the time and the second thing never.

As long as we're putting it all out there—here are several things I'm well aware are wrong with me.

A major flaw keeping me from being 100 percent likable by women is that I full-on don't recycle. I just haven't embraced it. I won't go more than 1 percent out of my way to participate in what I realize is an incredibly important group effort toward our children's future. It isn't that I'm ignorant or don't get why we're doing it. No, I know, I just don't do it. It's a total scumbag move, and I get it. Yet if I need to discard a giant plastic bottle and there isn't an already extremely organized recycling effort all clearly marked for me . . . that fucker is going straight into the trash. You know what makes it ironic? I worked on the back of a recycling truck for six fucking summers. I literally recycled for a living day in and day out, every single day for six summers in a row. As soon as I got home? Chug a Diet Coke and toss it in with the trash, feeling no shame.

Women don't like that I'm not very emotional. I personally disagree with this assertion, because I've cried several times in recent memory—most recently while watching *The Lion King*. Still, at this point, it's my vote versus every woman I've ever been involved with. I'm greatly outnumbered, so logic tells me I should concede the point and admit a couple of my emotional switches are janky. I like to think of myself more as emotionally grounded rather than emotionally absent. And sure, maybe I'm a little selfish when it comes to emotional stuff, too. For instance, if someone I know is going to die, I'd prefer they do it right after New Year's Day. January and February are great months to grieve. I basically have no plans then. Don't die on me in June, when things are about to heat up socially. I can't grieve through Memorial Day weekend; be reasonable.

But my worst flaw is that I farted on a baby once. Guilty as charged, folks. Don't get all high and mighty, like who is this pig who farts on babies? It can happen to anyone. Tornados can happen to anyone, too, and no one gets mad at them (besides Helen Hunt in *Twister*), because they are a part of nature, just like a mid-commute fart. Tornados take babies sometimes. This wasn't nearly as bad, so let's be thankful the baby remained unharmed, physically. I was walking to work from the Upper East Side to Midtown. I never wanted to live on the Upper East Side, but I had to temporarily move there after Big Sex dumped me. The walk is 1.3 miles and takes about twenty-two minutes. On the day in question, I had a really nice suit-tie combo on, my headphones were in, and my "spring into 2013" mix was peaking. I was in the homestretch, coming down Third Avenue, when I ran into your classic New York City commuter pickle. After commuting to and from work by foot for five-plus years, I understand what NASCAR is like. If you see your hole, you better *hit it*. There is nothing worse than getting caught behind a slow commuter, or even worse—a couple of fat tourists. There are no fat people living in Manhattan. That's a fact. People vary in size, but no one is actually fat. If you see fat people in front of you, you're stuck behind tourists. That's the pedestrian equivalent of being stuck behind a school bus.

Back to the scene. In front of me was a lady pushing a baby in a stroller at a respectable pace. She was moving at a decent clip, but I was late and needed to make a pass. There was someone coming the other way, but I still had a small window to make my move. It was so small, in fact, that it required me to turn my hips sideways while still facing forward, a little maneuver I like to call the "Stangle Shuffle." All the men in my family know it well; it's learned early in the world of giants. It consists of a forward-moving walk with the hips and torso rotating from side to side in order to squeeze through tight spaces. When you get really good at it, you can do it with a beer in each hand. At that point, you've learned to communicate with a unique system of head nods. It is most often executed at large crowd events such as concerts, house parties, and Tea Party rallies. In this particular case, on the sidewalk of Third Avenue, I executed the perfect Stangle Shuffle to gain a better position on the sidewalk. As my hips were turned right and I was in midstride, mid-pass, I did something else that all Stangle men learn at an early age—I let out a duck fart. A rip-roaring duck fart, guys. It went directly onto the baby I was passing. My immediate thought was that the baby was going to start crying. I farted on my little cousin once, years ago when he was six. He cried pretty hard. He was such a little pussy. I can't remember when I was six, but I'd like to think that I would have found that funny. It's not like I gave him a facial; that would have been way more fucked-up. The baby seemed okay, though. I guess you can't really judge when you shit yourself four times a day with butt mud. The mom, though? She wasn't as forgiving. We had ourselves a long conversation about it.

I am usually pretty good in awkward situations. Some would say awkward is my natural medium. One time, I went on a first date, and it went really well. I brought the girl back to my apartment and she absolutely fell in love with my dog, Frank. We took him for a quick walk around the block, so he could do his thing before I made my move. He got outside and immediately took a huge dump. In that huge dump was a used condom he had found in my trash and decided to eat the night before. Try explaining *that* one.

Some of my most awkward moments happen when I'm by myself. It's why I don't think I could ever get married. If anyone was around me when some of this stuff happens to me, I'd be toast. Recently, I had just bought some new clothes, and I was in my fudgies (underwear), trying them on in front of the mirror at my apartment. I put this one new shirt on and looked at my reflection and confidently said out loud, "Fuck yeah, I look hot." Then, when I turned to take it off and fold it, I let out a rip-roaring fart and just completely sharted. You know you sharted before you even feel it, because of the distinct sound it makes. I didn't feel so hot anymore. It was time to enter cleanup phase. I looked like Danny DeVito as the Penguin, walking across my apartment to the bathroom. Twenty minutes before all of this happened, I had hung up a few semi-wrinkled garments in the bathroom, cranked the shower as hot as it would go to get a good steam going, and shut the door (a great move when you're in a pinch, by the way). So when I opened the door, I could barely let the steam escape before plunging down on the john. It was a jungle, my friends.

Freshly sharted, I took an explosive shit in a very moist sauna. I'm dripping head to toe in sweat, possibly suffering the effects of dehydration. I actually had been avoiding looking to my right, where the TP is kept, because there could be a chance we were out of TP and at that point, well, I might lose it. It comes in threes! I very much need to get into the shower, face opposite the showerhead, and do my best Vince Wilfork three-point stance for the next few hours. Good night!

Punched by a Midget, Directly in My Penis

(Dave)

If our dad ever reads this book (which he won't), this may be the only chapter he enjoys. Our dad doesn't read books like this. He reads books about Abe Lincoln or books by Bill O'Reilly. He recently read a book *about* Abe Lincoln *by* Bill O'Reilly. That's a fact. Should someone slip an Abe Lincoln book cover over this book to trick him, and should he open to this very chapter, he may actually read it. For some reason, of everything to pick from, our dad finds this story to be his favorite. It involves several elements that old men love: bar fights, midgets, and humiliated sons. Since the title gives away the ending, I'm not spoiling anything by saying that our old man was laughing about this incident before I even had the ice pack on my wiener. You'd think a guy with a mule for a dick would feel some sympathy for me. Nope.

In 2008 I was young, fresh out of college, ambitious, and full of wonder. I was carrying around a *bachelor's* degree, dick swinging, just tickling the world to get it laughing before I was ready to finger it. I was studying to take the LSAT and working several part-time jobs. At first, I was the manager at Gilgo Beach in Long Island.[1] That job was sick, but it wasn't ideal for studying. When I wasn't ogling one of the high school girls who worked for me (relax, I was twenty-three . . . ish), I was getting high behind a lifeguard stand. Keep in mind lifeguard stands are not enclosed structures that provide privacy from those you don't wish to see you get high. They are a couple of two-by-fours, with a bench at the top. It didn't even make sense! I needed my days to study and my nights to make enough money, so I ended up getting a job as a doorman at a club called the Nutty Irishman in nearby Bay Shore, Long Island. This place was an absolute disaster. To every chin-strap-wearing, flat-brim-hat-sporting, old-Acura-with-tinted-windows-driving Long Island dickhead, this was his mecca. It was also the bar closest to where the Fire Island ferry lets off. With the last ferry leaving Fire Island at 1 a.m., we became the spillover for Pauly D and the gang to come drink Heinekens. I'm six four, at the time probably weighed about 230 pounds, and I was *by far* the smallest bouncer at the bar. These guys were washed-up football players, prison yard guards, gym coaches, and prison yard gym coaches. They were monsters. One of the guys actually told me a story about how he killed someone

---

1   The marshy stretch between Gilgo Beach and neighboring Oak Beach would later dominate the news as the decomposed remains of several missing prostitutes started turning up one by one. The culprit was never found, though I'd like to take this opportunity to assure our readers I had nothing to do with dumping those bodies. I love hookers!

in Queens once. Because of my whiteness and relatively pussy persona compared to the other bouncers, I acquired the nickname "Little Dave." When it came time to get rough, I was always given mop-up duty. When two meat-heads wanted to charge each other like rhinos, it was the real bouncers who would do suplexes and sleeper holds. While they were laying down T-bones and full nelsons, I would hold back their girlfriends. I became the butt of just about every joke. I loved it, though. These giant knuckle-heads embraced me for being so little. That was a first.

The Nutty Irishman used to have live bands every Saturday. They stuck with mostly local groups, but once in a while they would have a band with some sort of gim-mick: all-girl bands, cover bands, you know the drill. One night, they booked this band that was an all-midget KISS cover band. Fucking awesome. I would usually get to work early to help stock the bar. This allowed me an opportunity to steal a bottle of well liquor to bring out to the front door with me for the night. That night, I saw the midget KISS guys unloading and setting up. Full makeup, little tiny fellas. They went all-out. As the night started, I realized that this midget band had a *huge* midget following. Midgets from all over were turning up. Do you know how hard it is to keep it together when you have to ask hundreds of midgets for ID? They are so insulted. They kept looking at me like what, you think I chalked my midget ID? You think a fellow of-age midget passed his ID down to me? Check the height. It says four feet three. Fucking measure me, you punk! Also, I either had to say, "look up at me, please" or I would have to squat down to see their actual faces. This became extremely awkward, which I fully embraced. Oddly, they didn't find the humor in it.

As the night went on, I'd estimate we had about seventy-five midgets in this bar. We also had the usual crowd in there—the drunk idiots of Long Island. This was the ultimate recipe for a disaster. When midgets are in packs and drinking, they think they can fight regular people. This isn't the case. Every twenty or thirty minutes on my headset, I would hear about a small skirmish. I wanted to see one of my giant coworkers toss a midget out the door by his collar and the seat of his pants. It would have been too perfect. It never happened, though. Instead, we kept throwing out the full-size guys and leaving all the little guys inside. It was their night, after all. No reason to bring the fight to the street. At about 2 a.m., I got the order to close the front door. There was a full-blown brawl inside. I shut the door and headed in to see if I could help. It was mayhem. Imagine a swarm of midgets all working in a group to fight anyone who fucked with them. They were like a pack of hyenas jumping all over elephants, biting at their ankles.

In the history of Earth, there's been no manual written on how to handle this. I don't blame the midgets for being so fired up. These meatheads had been making fun of them all night. I had, too, but my jokes were cheeky and delightful. Theirs were mean and reflected their own insecurities. After a few minutes, I saw that there was a leader of the midgets who was clearly not backing down. He was fucking fearless; slippery, too. The bar was so crowded and he was so little, none of the giant bouncers could get ahold of him. He was just bobbing and weaving under skirts and around bar stools, causing trouble. Of course, Little Dave got assigned to him. The bouncer who killed a guy once, he told me to get the little guy the fuck out of here, so things would calm down. I felt like I was chasing around a squirrel that got in the house. He was scurrying everywhere. When I finally cornered him, I was exhausted. And confused. What, do I just pick him up like a kid? Hold him against my chest with my arm under his butt like a five-year-old? The only thing I could think to do was shoo him out. I began walking him toward the door with my hands and arms slightly out to my side, making a sweeping motion toward the exit. He was fairly cooperative as he walked backward, constantly looking around both sides of my hips, yelling at anyone who had something to say. My shoo method was working. As I walked forward and he walked backward, there was only about a foot between us. He recognized that he was on his way out, but he wanted to get in every word he could before we reached the door. When we were in the homestretch, someone did something that really, really didn't go over well: dumped a full pint of some sort of daiquiri directly on his oversized midget head.

He made a charge to get past me, and I deflected him back. I stood between him and the culprit. He tried again, and again I deflected him. Then that sneaky little fuck shrugged, rolled his eyes as if he were about to give up, then wound up and landed a haymaker directly on my junk. I dropped to my knees. I couldn't fucking believe it. He sprinted past me and dove into the crowd like Scrooge McDuck diving into his vault of gold coins. I didn't know what happened to him, and I didn't care. The entire bar was filled with brawling meatheads and midgets, and I was crawling on the ground, unable to grasp what had happened. Somehow, the fight died down and was wrangled under control within two minutes of all this happening. The band stopped playing, cops showed up, the dust was settling.

A pain- and whiskey-induced blackout has kept me from remembering much from the rest of the night, but what I can tell you is that the Nutty Irishman had a shitload of security cameras. After the bar closed that night and the staff remained, we enjoyed a multi-angle, *SportsCenter* highlight-style replay of my dick's encounter with a midget fist. I'm not sure what happened to that footage, but I'm definitely going to try to get a copy for my old man. He'd appreciate that.

Gay Guys,
They're Awesome!

We Honestly Wish We Were

(Mike)

You know where gay guys love hanging out? Vacation towns. And Washington, D.C. It just so happens that I've spent the last couple of years bouncing between a few vacation towns and had a nice stint in D.C. Maybe it's my fashion-forward attitude, maybe I'm naturally approachable, most likely I'm just way too comfortable with my sexuality. Whatever the reason, I've been propositioned by gay men more times than I could count.

I'm not gay, but I do have several gay friends. How do I maintain this sexually *comfortable* balance? Let's just say I've had some practice. Before I even get into this whole subject, let me make it completely clear that most gay guys are fucking awesome. *Every* group has a coupla dickheads, but for the most part, I enjoy my time with the gay dude demographic. In fact, I would make a great gay guy—save one massive characteristic: I don't like dick! Dave and I have had this conversation several times and are in complete agreement. If we didn't like girls so much, think about it . . . gay guys (generally) dress cool, throw fabulous parties, can cook, are cultured, have tons of girlfriends, can dance, have interesting hobbies, are in great shape . . . I mean come on, those fellas really TCOB.

Dave is probably 30 percent gay, which still doesn't qualify him as gay, but he's closer than I am (so jealous). The other day we started talking about gay guys, and I got thinking back to my Math B Algebra days, and came up with this "proof." (Remember those? I don't. Just had to google what they were called.)

(Male)sexdrive + (male)sexdrive >
(male) sexdrive + (female)sexdrive =
gay guys are *way* hornier.

No good at math? Me neither. The bottom line is that guys generally have a stronger sex drive than most women. Women just aren't built with semen in them. They don't need to *get it out* every goddamn day. When you get two guy-loving-guys together, they're going to be much randier than if there was a boner-buzzkill in the mix. Add to this the fact that they don't even understand monogamy. Bet you my bottom dollar that gay guys cheat more, but they don't even consider it cheating—it's more like "boys' night out."

When a husband ends a marriage on the excuse that he is gay and wants to have sex with men, everyone says,

"Good for you! You came out! You found yourself. You are honest." If a straight guy ends a marriage because he wants to have sex with women, he's an asshole. My point here is that claiming you're gay *might* be the best excuse to get out of marriage. Even if it means actually going gay for a little while, you still get out of a shithole marriage, and people actually support you! They'd probably even buy you things, help get you started on your new, gay life. You'd start dressing better, probably get in shape, you'd definitely start tipping better. Before you know it, you're a new man! A new, gay man. I guess I don't really know the endgame with this one. You'll just have to let your conscience be your guide.

Mark

Want a formula for a can't-miss night? Pair up a straight guy you can't make uncomfortable (me) with a butt-hugger you can't offend. Meet my friend Mark: he is twice my age and a titan of his industry. Mark and I met through my roommate Slime Dog, who knows Mark through work. Mark is a high-profile, consummate professional and an avid dick sucker. Mark and I both like joking around, making people a little uncomfortable, and we both get a kick out of pushing the envelope every once in a while. It is these shared characteristics that have built an overnight friendship.

Upon meeting Mark one fateful Thursday during a D.C. happy hour, our group found itself in a very nice, very gay steak house. Until arriving there, I didn't even realize there was such a thing as a gay steak house, but Mark clearly did. What excellent service! Claude, our server, was a delight.

It was Slime Dog, gay Mark, and smart-hot but sort-of-bitchy Asian Kara (Slime Dog's other coworker), and myself. The four of us had some gay drinks and ordered some gay steaks, then looked around and started to giggle about the situation we found ourselves in. Slime Dog and Kara were sitting next to each other and looked as though they were a couple. Mark and I were across from them, so I looked like Mark's boy toy. The clientele was old, rich, and hungry for meat. I took a look around and realized these guys were looking back. I'd never had such a captive audience. Ninety percent of the room was looking at Mark like he was the luckiest guy in the world. Shit started getting weird when a group of eight or ten older guys eating together next to us were entirely turned around in their chairs to stare at me (this is a goddamn *restaurant*). All I could do was laugh.

After about five old-fashioneds, I was confident that I simply *could not* offend Mark. Every time the jokes got rolling, especially the gay ones, he would one-up me immediately. This makes sense; I guess he's had practice. It was around that fifth old-fashioned that I brilliantly realized my new gay friend would be pivotal in introducing me to the girl of my dreams. Girls love gay guys! The only problem was, we were in a place inhabited almost completely by penises. Seriously, I felt like I was walking a runway when I had to use the restroom. It kind of boosted my confidence, is that weird?

The old-gay-gawkers left eventually, and a group of women replaced them. These gals were beauties, *all of them*. Except one, whatever. We were getting ready to leave and Mark drunkenly offered to introduce me to this entire table of pretty girls. I obviously agreed and approached with Mark, full of inflated confidence. Mark introduced me and I got a warm reception; these gals were sweethearts! We ended up sitting down for a drink with them, having a bunch of laughs and taking a few photos. Whoa, Mark is my secret weapon! How did this strategy for meeting nice girls not occur to me sooner? Photos taken, drinking, laughing, joking, they're sorta touchy-feely, incredible eye contact! What is happening?!

Oh, wait. They thought I was gay. Of course they weren't threatened. Well, I guess that ship sailed.

We eventually go to the next place, a bar on the other side of town. It's me, Slime Dog, gay Mark, and smart-hot but sort-of-bitchy Asian Kara. It's eleven thirty, we're already shitfaced, and nobody is ready to switch from bourbon to beer. So we spend a messy three or four hours gallivanting around D.C. Slime Dog's looking for love, Kara's being hot but kind of bitchy, but also kind of funny, and Mark's drunk enough to start feeling out if I'm like secretly gay or something. We trade jokes for an hour, and I finally convince him I genuinely like women. At this point, I am so drunk, all I can manage to do is tell him that I "wasn't a butt hugger." After I make the not-liking-dick thing as clear as I can, Mark gets on this kick of introducing me to women who are CLEARLY out of my league. Model-type women, gals with boyfriends standing next to them, unfriendly black hotties. None of them go home with me, but we certainly have entertained ourselves.

It's 4 a.m. and Slime Dog goes home with a nice gal, we put Kara in a cab, and I tell Mark I'm walking the ten minutes home to the studio I share with Slime Dog. Mark says he'll walk with me, then hop into a cab outside my place. We stumble to my building and he asks to use my bathroom, drunkenly promising he "won't try and fuck me." I take my new friend at his word, and we head upstairs—just a straight twenty-four-year-old intern and a gay fifty-year-old executive, pallin' it up. He ends up hanging out for a drink, and next thing I know, it's 8 a.m. . . . I wake up, still drunk. I'm in the recliner and look over to see Mark all curled up, boots on, in my bed. I laugh, jump over to Slime Dog's bed, and pass out with a smirk on my face. A few hours later, I wake up to Slime Dog (literally) shitting his pants laughing. He had arrived home in the early morning and was hungover, getting a drink from the kitchen. He heard boots coming out of the bathroom and figured I met someone the night before, and that I consequently had a girl over. Instead, the person he actually saw exiting his bathroom was his gay consultant, Mark.

Mark hung out for a while and eventually made his

exit. Slime Dog often still wonders aloud about my true sexuality. As I'm writing this, Mark and I are texting plans to get drunk sometime next week. He's definitely going to try to fuck me again. I can't wait!

Randy

I was living in Steamboat Springs, Colorado. At night, I worked at this bar right on the mountain called Slopeside, and I taught ski lessons during the day. One afternoon, I'm really high, skiing on my own, and I get talking to this guy on the chairlift. He's my father's age, friendly, standard. We chat about what we do, and my ski instructing comes up. By the end of the chairlift ride, he asks me for a lesson off the books. You see, a private lesson through the mountain is $650—it's crazy steep for the customer, and the instructor only sees about $100 of that. He wants to ski trees and moguls better, and he offers me $200 cash for a lesson. I agree, obviously.

We meet the next morning around nine to start the lesson. This guy, Randy, is awesome! A salesman from Philly, he owns a condo here with his wife and spends three or four weeks a year in the mountains. I'm a bit hungover for the lesson, and he sympathizes during our funny conversation about being young, drinking, and shenanigans. We get through a whole day of skiing, and boy is it a beauty! The weather is perfect; he's a good skier and a really good dude, to boot. At one point he even gets me high in the woods. This is the last guy on the planet that I would expect to indulge in that sort of hippie stuff.

At the end of the lesson, he offers to buy me lunch, a move that is nice but not that uncommon for customers to do. I oblige and suggest we go to my bar, which we can ski to and where we will be treated well. I introduce him to coworkers and my boss, and all is well in the world. Just as salads are served, we get into a talk about patriotism, of all things.

"I'm a big flag flyer," he says. "Five or six American flags around the house."

Sorta strange, but whatever floats your boat. An old-guy hobby, I suppose.

Me: Nice, funny you should mention, I have a pair of American flag print swim trunks.

Randy: Oh they sound nice. . . . Are they Speedos?

Me: Uh . . . what?

Randy: I just think you'd look nice in a Speedo. . . . So, do you have hairy legs?

Me: Wha—uh . . . not more than norm . . . what?

Holy shit . . . Is this guy . . . He could be my grandfather . . . Wait, did he pay me yet?

Randy: Well, by now you must know. I'm interested in you sexually. Do you feel the
same way toward me?

Me: Uh . . . excuse me? No, man. Sorry. You're
barkin' up the wrong tree. . . . I wish I
could help you. Wait! I don't wish I could
help you. I just wish you the best of . . .
God damn it! Sorry, man, I like vagina, to
put it bluntly.

Randy: Really?

*What does he mean by really?! Why is he surprised?
Man, this is happening too much. I need to start looking
tougher. . . . I can't even leave, he hasn't paid me yet!
Did he even need a lesson? Probably a lesson in dude
fuckin' . . .*

Me: No, sir, sorry. Not a dick guy. I'm not
uncomfortable or anything, just want
to make clear I am *not* interested in you
sexually. . . .

Randy: No problem! I'm a salesman, you know!
Had to ask . . . But really, you wouldn't
even have to do anything, just sit
there. . . .

Me: Oh-Jesus-God-no! Randy, stop that. Seriously, vagina for me. Come on, dude.

Randy: Okay, last time. Sorry. Anyways . . .

What the fuck do we talk about for the remaining forty-five minutes of this meal? Does this mean he won't tip me? Should I give him a sympathy HJ? Seriously, Mike, too soon.

Me: So . . . you're gay, huh? What's that like?

Maybe it's the result of living in more socially progressive cities after growing up in a small town, but we're both genuinely thankful we're part of a generation that has actually seemed to let go of the stigma surrounding homosexuality. Nobody in our generation seems the least bit worried about which body part makes you antsy in your pantsy, and that is fantastic news. If in your spare time you'd prefer to butt-hug your buddy instead of bedding a nice lady—it doesn't matter to me. Nobody we know that's our age is worried about gay marriage. Dave and I are lucky to have as many hilarious, fabulous, dick-loving friends as we do. Haaaaaay!

The Gag Is Up!

(Dave)

I've got no problem with the vegetarians. I've got no problem with the vegans. As a person who generally abuses my body like a stepchild, I admire people who monitor what they put in their bodies. All of you health nuts will eventually have the *best* breast milk; kudos. I'm basically the opposite, though. I put nearly everything imaginable in my body, take note of which of those things gives me pleasure, then load up those things as much as possible. I have zero discipline whatsoever. How do you vegetarians do it? How many slaughterhouse videos and crushes on your bearded Anthropology 101 professor did it take to say you'll never eat any sort of meat again? Do what you've got to do, you hot little hippie—it sort of turns me on. Hippies are more liberal under the sheets, and they love getting high. That's right in my wheelhouse! Just put a *little* bit of effort into shaving *some* parts of your body once in a while, and you and I will be cooking with Crisco.

What I do have a problem with is when you hippie vegetarians decide that following your own dietary no-nos isn't enough, and now everyone else must go along with them. That's where I draw the line. Every red-blooded American deserves three things in this world:

1. A fair election

2. Getting out of one DUI scot-free

3. A goddamn hamburger without a side of someone else's unsolicited progressive views

I went to high school with this gal who was a die-hard vegetarian. If vegetarianism were Christianity, this girl would have been an apostle. Her name was Moonbeans. Moonbeans was a great girl—funny, smart, and cute. Great butt, too. At one point, she developed a really intense crush on me that took our friendship somewhere weird. I remember on Christmas Eve my senior year of high school she sent me a text message (which cost me twenty-five cents at the time; so selfish) alerting me to a letter she left in my mailbox. I opened the mailbox to find an envelope stuffed full of paper. She had written me a seventeen-page letter. Front and back. Handwritten. I knew it meant a lot to her, and she must have poured her seventeen-year-old heart into it. Poor thing. I also remember that later on that night, I was drunkenly reading it aloud to a rowdy dinner table crowd of aunts, uncles, cousins, and friends. Halfway through, I was completely exhausted from laughing. I was doing this really funny impression of her while reading it; the table was eating it up. Still, that letter had some heart. I think she might have dotted every *i* and *j* with a heart. The meat of the message focused on her belief that we were destined to be together.

I knew all too well I wanted nothing to do with Moonbeans on a romantic level. It was just bad chemistry. I didn't help the situation by occasionally getting horizontal with her when we'd both had a few too many Zimas. It was high school, people, things got weird. It made it harder to get the point across that she and I were way too different. If we were at a barbecue, we'd always have to have a separate grill for whatever piece of weird tofu she brought for herself, and somehow I was always the one getting an earful about it. She gave me so much shit about it throughout high school that it made me start to resent all vegetarians. I think I ate *more* meat because of it, just to spite her. In the earlier years, I would try to trick her into eating meat by concealing it in mashed potatoes. I made up erroneous facts about the mental health effects of not eating meat. I remember telling her that women who don't get nutrients from animal protein tend to develop hair around their nipples. As a side note, this is how I was first able to get her to show me her tits (so on point). They were fantastic, by the way.

Sometimes we'd make flirtatious bets revolving around a "meat-in-your-mouth" sort of theme. Those were fun. Our senior year of high school, our group of friends went to Pizza Hut Buffet for lunch once a week. For those of you who don't know what Pizza Hut Buffet is, it's Pizza Hut plus Buffet. Arguably my three favorite words all rolled up into one incredible experience: PHB. Five dollars got you unlimited 'za, bread sticks, and salad. BOOM! At one point, they even served draft beer. It didn't last long, though. It was too good to last long. I think God must have just noticed how great a deal it was and felt He needed to avoid a massive population spike around the Albany, New York, Pizza Hut branch, so He had them tone it down. Mysterious ways, I get it.

There at PHB, Moonbeans and I were sitting at the opposite ends of a long table with several of our friends between us. Looking back on high school Dave, I was probably wearing a button-down that was way too big on me and some nice boot-cut jeans, comfort waist. Are there any pants in the world more tailor-made for a PHB sesh than wide leg, comfort waist jeans, you guys? I was betting Moonbeans that I could throw a piece of sausage off my pizza (fifth slice not counting dessert pizza, which was also a thing) and into her open mouth from where I was sitting. She was about fifteen feet away. The terms were that if I made the sausage throw into her mouth on my first shot, she had to chew and swallow it. After I convinced her I had such little chance at hitting the shot that the risk was worth the entertainment value, she agreed. She didn't think about how big beer pong was back then, and how the same basic motion of throwing a sausage chunk into a mouth had been practiced, by me, for ten thousand hours around beer pong tables every Friday and Saturday night.

I pulled up, took aim, and let one fly. This is where

you assume I hit it, nothing but tongue. Game over. No re-rack needed. Nope—not the case, my friends. IT HIT THE CORNER OF HER MOUTH and fell to the table. Total. Fucking. Heartbreaker. I'm sorry to let you down, gang. What's more important, and the reason I'm taking you back to the PHB that night, is that moments after the commotion went down, as the bill was being paid and the chicks were playing on their Motorola Razr phones and picking out what mix CD they were going to listen to on the way home, I saw something very peculiar out of the corner of my eye. As no one was paying attention, I could have *sworn* I saw Moonbeans at the end of the table reach her little hand out, sneakily pick up the sausage chunk, and pop it right into her mouth. I exploded! I jumped up on my chair and started exclaiming like Oral Roberts at a tent revival! I couldn't believe what I saw! Moonbeans, the greatest vegetarian of all time, was a sham! Imagine seeing Gandhi sneak some naan during a hunger strike! Imagine Al Gore cranking his AC when he's not even home! Imagine cats and dogs, *living together*! Of course, she denied it and everyone believed her; it was too big a story to expose without evidence. Plus, I was acting like a fucking lunatic. No one believed me, but now I knew the goddamn truth. You had us all fooled, Moonbeans.

Throughout our friendship, we made out a few times; we did some stuff that teenagers do. It was one of those "yeah, I gotta go" types of things where we knew we were playing with fire, but we gave in every once in a while. I didn't need any more seventeen-page letters, and she wasn't getting the message. I hated the idea of me letting it go too far, because I knew she was a great person and at the time had a *real* thing for me. Seventeen pages' worth. It became increasingly difficult for me to hang around with her and not hook up with her. What's worse, I was so obsessed with my conspiracy theory about her being a fake vegetarian that I couldn't stop hanging out with her. Years later, when season one of *Homeland* came out, I thought Showtime might have been basing Carrie's character on me. As I got deeper and deeper into my investigation, I found we were ending up under the sheets more and more. These drunken flings carried on for a few months, and I started to notice things about her. One time while camping out in the Adirondacks (as you do in upstate New York), we were making out against a tree in the middle of the afternoon. How cool does that sound? I noticed that her breath smelled like bacon. I thought it was my breath, because I had just housed a pound of it, but this was different. This was girl-bacon-breath, if that makes any sense? Another time on a ski trip, I was certain I tasted chili on her lips. We had a huge pot of it going at the house, and people were helping themselves all afternoon. The circumstantial evidence was piling up; my theory was starting to hold water. Soon after, I began openly accusing her of being a fake vegetarian. I had little to no support. After all, I had been making things up about her hairy-nippled vegetarian lifestyle for years, to anyone who would listen.

This boy had cried wolf one too many times. Without the smoking gun, no one believed me. It was entertaining and all, but we're talking about the vegetarian Joan of Arc.

All of this vegetarian conspiracy mumbo jumbo came to a head the summer after our senior year. It was your classic carefree high school get-together. It was a mix between *Dazed and Confused* and *Wet Hot American Summer*. We barbecued all day up at the lake, we drank a thousand Busch Lights, the best beer ever, and everyone was wearing bikinis. It was an old-school high school shindig. Moonbeans and I were even getting along pretty well. I cooked a ton of chorizo for the gang just to spite her, but made sure to keep it to just one half of the grill so she could fire up some strange roots or whatever the fuck. We drank, swam, and fooled around in a cabin. I dare you to name me a better scenario. Things got *so* high school in the top bunk after dinner one night. I think she was appreciative of me keeping the chorizo to the carnivore side of the grill earlier on, and she wanted to show some gratitude. Now, keep in mind we were in high school, so when she did go down on me, she had no idea what she was doing. Blowjobs were so funny then, everything was an experiment. It was like ordering ceviche at a restaurant—just completely different every time. Remember in *Jurassic Park* when that cowardly lawyer runs away from the kids and hides in the Porta-John? Then the T. rex smashes that Porta-John to smithereens, leaving the lawyer exposed with his pants down and the

T. rex just chomps down on his entire torso and shakes it side to side? That's what this girl did to my high school peener. Another night, again after too many Zimas, she started to really push the boundaries. I'd normally suspect she had possibly been watching some porn, but this was 2003, so that would have caused a busy signal for hours on AltaVista. I guess she must have just found some confidence with what she was doing. As she started pushing it more and more, I heard some uncomfortable noises coming from below the Mason-Dixon, almost like she was struggling. They continued to get more intense as the act progressed toward its final sequence. I didn't know she was in over her head until it was too late. She got sick all over me. You can't just completely ignore a gag reflex when you've been boozing, Moonbeans, and now we've just made a complete mess of me. Somehow, I think she was too drunk to be mortified. This gave me some relief, as I could now stop concentrating on consoling an embarrassed high school girl and instead focus on *cleaning puke and semen off my favorite 30 percent of my body*. I should mention that there was a house party going on outside the room. All our friends, on whom I had been pushing the conspiracy theory, were outside.

I hurried into the bathroom to assess the damage. It was bad down there. I started with paper towels, which were immediately rendered useless. I moved on to real towels, but that was just mean to the towels. They'd never be the same. I decided that a shower was the only thing that could work. As I was undressing and separat-

ing my clothes and the towels into two piles (one free of
puke and semen, the other covered in it), I noticed something. I noticed her puke, its color and its consistency.
It had a yellowish hue with small chunks of brown and
red. They stood out to me, I couldn't figure out why. I
hopped into the shower and started rinsing off. The mess
came off my skin but the mental image of her barf could
not escape my thoughts. Yellow, brown, red. Yellow,
brown, red. Goo. Chunks. Goo-chunks. What did she
eat? What was in her stomach? A kaleidoscope of images
from the day began rapid-firing in my head as the water
rushed over me. Beer. Camp. Fire. Grill. Chorizo. Blowjob. Yellow. Brown. Red. Flashback of PHB in slow motion. Yellow. Brown. Red. All of a sudden a 10,000-watt
idea lightbulb clicked on above my head. Those brown
and red chunks were chorizo! Yes, ladies and gentlemen,
everybody's favorite pork sausage originating from the
Iberian Peninsula and featured earlier on my grill was
sitting in chunks, in a pile of vomit, on a towel on the
sink! Unless a man's penis is capable of digesting entire
chunks of meat and ejaculating them (yet to confirm
this), I had my evidence! She puked up some chorizo she
must have snuck earlier on in the night. I knew it! THIS
WAS MY MOMENT! I'm also just now realizing how ap-
propriate it was that my *penis* served as my smoking gun.
It was too perfect. I had to tell the world!

My first thought was that I wished I had yellow
crime scene tape. I didn't want *any* of the evidence disturbed; I couldn't have anyone contaminating the chain

of custody. I delicately folded the towel up and scurried out into the main party. By this time, Moonbeans had cleaned herself up and made a stealthy exit from the bedroom so as not to alert anyone that we were up to some funny business. Little did she know that her gag reflex was about to topple her entire hippie empire! I gathered everyone who would listen, and I resumed my role as prosecutor. I instantly became a courthouse sensation. I might have even developed a southern drawl? I drew in the audience with leading questions such as, *What did we all eat for dinner tonight?* into *And what color would y'all describe that meat as?* then combined it with a little *And what types of people don't eat meat?* with a bit of *And can anyone point to any known vegetarians in the room?* The stage was set for a showdown! As I took out exhibit A and unfolded my precious evidence, I took a look around the room at all the faces waiting eagerly for the big reveal and what it would all mean. I saw her friends shaking their heads in a "no way" fashion. I saw my friends nodding with approval. As I continued to scan, I saw Moonbeans staring back at me completely defeated. It was the first time I had ever seen that look on her face. For as long as I had known her, she had been strong, proud, and full of conviction. Even if she was a fake, at least she picked something she wanted to believe in and fiercely spread the message, whether she could measure up to it or not. Never once during her grill-side flip-outs or twenty-minute lectures did she show even a fraction of the vulnerability she was showing before the big reveal.

Was I assuming too much? Maybe. Was her vulnerability probably more rooted in how embarrassed she would be for people to find out that a babe like her was fooling around with a goof like me? Probably. But for that moment when our eyes met, I realized how far beyond me she was emotionally—how far I was from having *any* sort of cause even remotely as close to my heart as vegetarianism was to hers. Son of a bitch . . . I just couldn't do it. What did I do instead? I had convened and primed a jury of my peers, and now I had no exit strategy! All eyes were on me. People were hungry and wanted to get to their hot plates. I started to sweat. I used an extended pause, but it only generated more anticipation. Finally, I threw in the figurative towel. I claimed that my entire case had been an elaborate hoax to distract everyone from the fact that she threw up on my penis mid-blow-Johnson. I chose *a* real truth over *the* real truth. Was Moonbeans embarrassed? Sure. Was her cover as a fake vegetarian blown? Nope, safe and sound.

Have I Mentioned Quack?

"Like a Duck"

(Dave)

I've got a friend named Quack. Quack is tough to describe. If I start with his personality, it will take away from how bizarre he looks physically. If I start by describing his taste in women, you'll get violently ill before I get into how big a sweetheart he actually is. And if I start by describing how big a sweetheart he actually is, I'll be telling a bald-faced lie.

His introduction is always strong and throws people off right away. Quack. Quack? Why the fuck is his name Quack? Yet that is possibly the only easy thing to understand about him. Quack's full name is Ryan Grady Quackenbush. Aside from Mike and me, Quack is the only person whose true full name will appear unchanged in this book. It'd be borderline impossible to drag Quack's reputation through the mud any more than he's been doing since the day I met him. Ryan was a twelve-year-old fat kid, and Quack was his persona. "Hi," he'd say with his tiny little hand reached out for a dead-fish handshake, "Quack. Like a duck." He'd walk away before people knew what to think. That's still his move to this day. He knows people need a moment to digest not only what they are hearing, but also what they are seeing. Half the people who meet him for the first time probably aren't listening to a word he is saying. Quack is arguably the most uniquely shaped individual this world has ever known. He is quite rotund, to be frank. His body is almost a perfect sphere, actually. Add to that, he only stands at exactly five feet tall "on the nose," he'll have you believe. But I've maintained for years that he is actually only four feet eleven. The Quackenbushes, as a family, aren't the tallest bunch in the world. They're all short. They breed down, too. Every new generation of Quackenbush children is like opening up another Russian nesting doll to find an even smaller one inside. Quack is the shortest of the bunch. He is the little nugget at the very center.

Quack, told ya.

Quack's mother has become a world-class seamstress over the years, I'd imagine from having to always hem regular people clothes to fit her family of lawn gnomes. Seamstresses always have measuring tape around, so I stole a roll from his mom and carried it around with me for weeks waiting to plot my move. When we were seventeen, Quack exclusively drank Gatorade-and-vodka. It was the only thing he would ever drink. No beers, no cocktails, no literally-anything-we-could-get-our-hands-on-because-we-were-seventeen. Nothing but Gatorade-and-vodka. The sugar in this combination constantly left him with vicious hangovers. I jumped him and tried to measure him when he was in the midst of sweating his way through one of the worst of these hangovers. He was mowing grass in his back-yard, and I was smoking grass in mine. Moments after I finished, my dad came home and made me help him give our racist German shepherd a bath in the backyard. As we chased her around, cornered her, and tied her to a tree for her wash-down, I noticed how helpless she was. She gave in and let it happen. This would be the blueprint for how I would finally prove Quack's true height. Knowing it was Saturday morning and he would be mowing grass, it was the perfect opportunity. I didn't even hesitate when I got to his place. I hopped his fence, ran up behind him, and literally kicked him as hard as I could in the back. That was about as far as I got. I had this whole grand plan and all these dog-washing tactics I was going to use. I couldn't even pin him down! It was like wrestling the Kool-Aid man. I couldn't get my arms around him! I was an in-shape seventeen-year-old lacrosse player, and I lost a wrestling match to a five-foot punk named after a buoyant waterfowl. From that day on, he was incontestably five feet tall.

Have I mentioned that Quack is a sick fuck? Just as people are starting to accept what they are seeing with Quack's insane exterior, they begin to experience how deeply deviant he is on the inside. He is the most perverted man I've ever been around, and he makes absolutely no effort to hide it from anyone in his company. I think it's his way of putting people to the test right away. If he disgusts you, he figures that it was coming eventually, so you might as well end the conversation now. If you laugh, you'll love him forever. Right away, he puts you on his level. Within minutes of your first conversation he may reveal to you his preference for large nipples on a woman (*I don't want to be able to tell where the boob ends and the nipple begins*) or his personal rules he won't break (*I insist on being on top when I sixty-nine*). Even the way he compliments my mom is strangely off (*You look handsome today, Mrs. S*). I recently walked by him at a party and overheard him finishing a story. All I caught was ". . . she asked me what was on my penis, and I said nothing, babe, I just shaved my pubes into the shape of a GoPro. Can we drop it already?" He was talking to my aunt Loretta. At three in the afternoon, at a family barbecue. Quack is out to make himself laugh first and foremost; if others find him funny, it's an added bonus. One time for Halloween, he dressed as Ed Harris's character from *The Truman Show*. He wore round glasses, a backward Kangol hat, and a hands-free headset. He walked around screaming, "Cut the feed!" the entire night. He didn't break character once. Pretty much *no one* got it.

Have I mentioned Quack has almost killed me more than eight times? Many people have had near-death experiences in their lives. For a guy in his late twenties, I'm further down the wrong end of the bell curve than I'd like to admit, but I'm still breathing. I attribute that to Quack. Not the still breathing part, no way. That's blind luck, and I'm living on borrowed time. I mean, it's my position on the bell curve that I attribute to Quack. Anytime I've had the realization that I was in true danger, the one that gives you that funny feeling in your butthole, Quack has been by my side and responsible for getting us there. Most of these experiences have taken place far away from home. That's when things get the craziest. The way to get Quack in his wheelhouse is to go more than two hours away from home. Because Quack never flies anywhere, that would mean you've got a drive ahead of you. If it's with Quack, there will be a cooler overflowing with cold Coors Lights. It's a staple of any drive over two hours. Don't count on Quack to do the driving, though, not even in his own truck. He is there for one thing and one thing only: to crush Coors Lights at an alarming rate. Quack has only owned (and will ever own) pickup trucks. He'll claim it's because he is a construction worker. That's bullshit. He won't drive a car because a car doesn't have a truck bed to dispose of empty Coors Light cans in with a toss over your shoulder while opening the next one. His truck bed looks like Scrooge McDuck's giant vault of gold, except it's filled with silver . . . bullets, that is.

In the spring of 2012, our friend Lance Bass was graduating from law school and having a party to celebrate what was a monumental feat among my group of friends. Our high school graduation parties were wild, not because we were proud of graduating from high school, but because we genuinely didn't know when the next time anyone in our group would ever graduate from another institution besides a federal penitentiary. Fast-forward eight years, and we've got a law school party on our hands? Fuck yes. Lance Bass pulled out all the stops, too. He rented a big house in Lake Placid, New York. In its history, that town had two things happen and two things only:

1. Host of the 1980 Winter Olympics, site of the "Miracle on Ice"

2. Host of Lance Bass's law school graduation party

Lake Placid won't let either of them go. The town is more than three hours away from where we grew up. Let's do the math. Three hours is more than two hours, and two hours qualifies us for . . . FULL COOLER. We hit the road at once. We were so antsy in the pantsy, we left at noon even though we weren't planning on pregaming for the pre-party that preceded the cocktail hour until at least five o'clock. It was a good thing we erred on the side of caution, too. About halfway between Albany and Lake Placid is Lake George. Remember Lake George? Sure you do. If you're passing through Lake George, you're not going to *not* stop in and experience the vibe a little, right? We thought we'd quickly grab lunch at Duffy's Tavern on the water, because it sounds like a bar that should be in *The Simpsons*, then maybe have one dog beer each (seven human beers) before hitting the road again.

I'm not sure how, and it's an entirely different story altogether, but Quack and I ended up playing nine holes of golf with two local fishermen we met at the bar. Have I mentioned Quack also has a vicious gambling problem? And he can't golf well at all? *We'll end up in the black,* he kept saying. Somehow, he was right. It's not shocking that two salty fishermen found his humor appealing. They were buying dog beers on the course like crazy, too. I think I had two dog beers. Before I knew it, we were back on the road after a quick four-hour pit stop. Now we were tuned up for a big night.

Quack and I rolled into Lake Placid at about 8 p.m., just as the cocktail hour was wrapping up. "I'm sorry, sir, the bar is closed, as the party will be moving upstairs for dinner now." It's not what we wanted to hear. Quack peeled off a hundred-dollar bill (I should mention Quack is the richest person I know and completely self-made; I know, right?) and all but shoved it down the poor bartender's throat as he told him *I didn't go through the trouble to put on this goddamn tie to hang out sober, compadre*. Quack had insisted we pack some suits for our trip, "Just in case we have to get buried up there." I think he was serious.

When we were about an hour out of town, we received word from the party that it was a swanky affair; attendees were suited up and wearing dresses. Have you ever taken off all your clothes and put on a full suit while driving a pickup truck with between two and three dog beers in you? The only thing harder is for Quack to do it. With his unique body type in play, he has developed an entire system for getting dressed. It's like watching a paraplegic get off his wheelchair to take a shit. There is grunting, sweating, a lot of arm work and breath control. Add in the confinements of a pickup truck at high speed and you can see how Quack had earned another drink. I went to the bathroom to take a much-needed pee and by the time I came back, Quack was in mid-handshake with the bartender as I heard, ". . . like a duck. Now, about those beers I need."

The remainder of the cocktail hour, dinner, and reception rolled on as expected. We were seated at the kids' table, while aunts and uncles looked at us with complete disgust. Every time the waitress walked by, Quack goosed her butt and asked for another round— even though she was there to deliver the current round. By the time dancing broke out, we were already climbing the scaffolding of the social guillotine. Lance Bass had this uncle who seemed to have a real problem with us.

Quack will tell you it was because I was getting handsy while dishing life advice to his uncle's eighteen-year-old daughter, who was set to attend Geneseo College that coming fall, my alma mater. That was only half of it, though. This red-faced uncle had a wife, too. She was short and thick and right up Quack's alley. When you're only five feet tall (allegedly), here is how your body stacks up to the average woman while dancing with her: your eyes are directly in line with her breasts, and your hands have nowhere to rest but on her ass. If you're looking to nudge a pissed-off uncle over the edge, Quack dancing with his wife is how you do it. We were coming at him from all angles: his young daughter getting the creep treatment from big Dave; his dear wife's butt getting kneaded like dough by a fat midget in a suit. A man can only take so much. He practically chased me out of the party, long before the party was over. I was all alone and had nowhere to go but to the bars in town.

Lake Placid has a lake in the middle of town. Weirdly, it's not Lake Placid but a smaller lake called Mirror Lake. On one side of Mirror Lake was Lance Bass's party, at which I was no longer welcome. On the other side are all the fun bars, my only consolation. Unless you have a boat, having a lake between you and your destination is a real pain in the dick. That's what I kept thinking as I was walking the perimeter of the lake in my suit, drunk and alone. When I was about halfway around it, I got a call from Quack. Shortly after I had been chased out of the party, Quack had his turn, too.

Have I mentioned Quack is a really fast runner for being so short and stubby? He can really scurry. It's saved his skin several times, and this was no exception.

When Angry Uncle was done with me, he came back in for Quack. Only, Quack put up a fight before he was chased out. He poked the bear just enough to give chase. From what Quack described, it sounded like the end of a *Benny Hill* episode with Angry Uncle chasing him all over town. Quack was calling me from some bushes and was desperate for a rescue. He said he could see Angry Uncle pacing in the streets in front of the party, yelling about the things he was going to do to us when he caught us. Meeting me on the road was a no-go. I told Quack to head down to the water, find a dock, and I'd take care of the rest. It was after midnight on a sleepy evening in Lake Placid. Logic suggested someone had to have a boat I could borrow to go rescue my friend. What's cooler than getting rescued by boat? Nothing. Maybe by helicopter, but I'd been drinking. It's not safe, you guys.

It's shocking how easy it is to steal a boat on Mirror Lake. There are tons of them all just floating there, ripe for the picking. One dock had two boats. The first was a speedboat, but I was confident it would wake up the nice folks I was borrowing it from. The second was a fifteen-foot pontoon boat with a stationary bike in the middle of it. It looked homemade. I hopped on to get a closer look. It turned out the stationary bike was hooked up to paddles underneath the pontoons. I'd like to imagine myself as more of a steal-the-speedboat kind of guy, but when I weighed grand larceny versus getting in a solid cardio burn, I'm happy to say I made the right choice. I had three dog beers to work off, after all.

This boat could move! It was a fucking blast. It was like I was taking a Spin class, but instead of being the fattest guy in the room, I was the *only* guy in the room, and the room was made of water. I called Quack again to tell him I stole a boat to rescue him with, and he should walk to the end of the dock. He had no follow-up questions. He simply whispered that I needed to *make haste*. I made haste, all right; I was fucking flying across that lake. I had discovered that the pedals had these Velcro foot straps that would prevent any slippage, real heavy-duty. By the time I got across the lake to Quack, I was an absolute pro with this boat. I almost wish there had been more boat traffic, so I could have demonstrated a textbook parallel park. I would have nailed it.

Quack had found the longest dock in the history of docks to wait on. It came out about seventy-five feet into the water. I figured he chose that dock because it gave him the most cover in the darkness of night. That cover was immediately blown as I pulled up to the end of the dock and Quack screamed, "Permission to come aboard?!" It didn't matter if Angry Uncle heard us from the shore, though, because this ship was leaving harbor! Quack was even emboldened to shout back to the shore about how *handsome* Angry Uncle's wife had been.

As I pedaled away from the dock, I noticed how

much harder it was with Quack on board. This vessel was clearly only built for one person. As I pedaled harder and harder, I knew something was off. We were going in circles, and I couldn't figure out why. I stopped and let the paddles underneath the pontoons come to rest. After trying to hear if something was broken, I noticed a fanning sound. *You hear that, Quack?* He wasn't paying attention. He had somehow gotten Angry Uncle's wife's phone number while dancing with her and was texting her about running away together. I did another pedal rotation, and the sound picked up. It was the right-side paddle. It had left the water and was up in the air. That was my first indication that the boat was beginning to tilt. My second indication was when the boat quickly started tilting. First, I felt it in my body, then I noticed it more as the right pontoon came completely out of the water. For some reason, Quack was still standing on the very corner of the boat, where he had hopped on. He was lost in his phone with a really fucked-up grin on his face. *Quack, move to the center of the boat.* No response. *Quack, this thing is tipping.* Still no response. Have I mentioned Quack is borderline illiterate? He gave up on reading and writing well before texting came along. As a result, he is forced to concentrate very, very hard while texting with a babe. Now we were really starting to tip. "QUACK!" I shouted. He looked up. "Hey, what's up Dave?" He said this as if he had just bumped into me for the first time that day. We tilted a little more and a little more and in an instant,

BOOM. The entire boat snapped completely upside down all at once. What kind of boat does that? A homemade one. Turns out guys who make their own boats don't run simulations on what would happen if they had a little meatball friend jump onto one corner. Quack was thrown into the water. I wasn't so lucky. Those Velcro straps I mentioned? They kept me right where I was as the boat flipped over on me. All of a sudden, Angry Uncle became the threat I was least worried about. I was strapped into a homemade boat that was capsized on top of me. Just as I thought the last of the boat owner's design flaws had showed its ugly head, I had to deal with one more.

I'm not exactly sure how this next part happened, so I can only assume that the guy who built the boat is either the biggest retard in the world *or* he built this feature in as an antitheft device for this very situation. Once the boat was upside down, the pontoons immediately filled with water and the boat sank on top of me. Mike and I grew up floating around on *The Entertainer*, a pontoon boat. We're freshwater guys! We get the physical laws of a pontoon. What. The. Hell?

By the time I got my feet unstrapped from the pedals, it was too late. I had a water-filled pontoon boat pinning me to the bottom of a lake. It was freak-out time for Dave. I tried lifting one side, then lifting the other. Way too heavy. I tried to summon that superhuman strength mothers get when they lift cars off babies. I'm not sure why that is such a universal example, as if cars are con-

stantly pinning infants to the ground in a race against
the clock, and the only option is for a mom to do a power
clean before the car crushes the baby more than it already has? Apparently this happens a lot? Those moms,
they find that strength from the love in their hearts. My
heart was filled with scorn and cholesterol. Soon it would
also be filled with lake water. That boat wasn't moving,
and I was starting to run out of air. My life completely
flashed before my eyes. I thought I was going to drown
on the bottom of Mirror Lake, in a full suit and tie, because I stole a boat to rescue my asshole friend who is
shaped like the Kool-Aid guy. I imagined the scuba div-
ers laughing as they found my body. I imagined the cops
having no idea where to begin when they explained it
to my parents. *Well, he was apparently doing some sort
of black-tie-only exercising in the middle of the night. . . .*
I imagined the Darwin Awards being renamed the Dave
Stangle Awards and every embarrassing death from then
on being compared to me, the ultimate retard. I imagined
what my tombstone would say.

DAVE STANGLE: 1984–2011

Complete Idiot. Dumber than Sticky,
the "Retarded Cat" (vet's phrase, not ours).

As I was ready to let it all go and succumb to the
cold waters, I decided to give it one more heave. This
time I planted my feet firmly on the sandy bottom of the

lake, did my best chair pose (yoga pays off, you guys) with the pontoons on my shoulders, and pushed with all my might. Nope. Nothing. Shit. Okay, time to die. Something *did* happen at the last second, though. One of the pontoons, being homemade and all, snapped under the combination of the water pressure pushing it down and me pushing it up. An enormous air bubble let out, as if Earth farted, and one side of the boat let up. FUCK. YES. I pushed off the bottom of the lake and rose like goddamn Godzilla. I ran out of air about five feet from the surface, inhaled about a gallon before I broke the plane, and coughed and choked my way over to the dock about fifteen feet away. I put my elbows up on the dock and choked up the last of the lake water I'd taken in. I was part choking, part coughing, part puking, and I *think* I might have even pooped a little bit? I'll admit that here.

When I finally got my bearings, my first thought was my dear old friend Quack. I looked around and there was no sign of him out in the water. What happened to him? Did he survive? Is he okay? Do I have to swim back down and pull his fat little body out from under the boat? God damn you, Quack, GOD DAMN YOU! I WON'T LET YOU DIE! NOT TONIGH—wait. Wait a second. What is that little blob sitting in the lifeguard chair onshore? Is that Quack? If it isn't, then it's the Penguin from *Batman*. Either way, I pulled myself up on the dock and ran in toward shore to see. There at the end of the dock in a soaking-wet suit was Quack looking down at his iPhone and tapping it, then holding it up to his ear, as if that were how you fix water damage to electronics. His first questions to me confirmed that Quack is a complete fucking lunatic: *What were you doing down there? No luck finding your phone? Mine's busted, too. Water's nice, though, right?*

Fudgies in Vegas

(Mike)

When Dave turned twenty-one, my family celebrated with a trip to Las Vegas. Our oldest brother, Sean, had moved out there a few years earlier, so it made perfect sense. At the time, I was only seventeen years old. Up until that point, getting away with drinking hadn't really been that much of a problem. I was seventeen, sure, but I was freakishly tall, with two older brothers who looked just like me. I was able to get away with more underage partying than most.

Dave (with a danglin' butt, sick move), Mike (posing hard, flexin' thigh like a boss), and Sean.

But not in Vegas. I didn't even come close. It's not even an option there. There is just way too much money, security, and beautiful hookers out there to even begin to fuck around with fake IDs. They have a hard enough time controlling the of-age folks; they have no time for underagers like me and Nick Papageorgio. The trip seemed like a wild time for everyone else, but it was downright boring for me. I spent a week (who goes to Vegas for a *week* anyway!?) riding a fucking roller coaster outside of our hotel, New York–New York, because that was pretty much the only thing I was allowed to do. On top of that, our hotel room faced the loudest part of the roller coaster. Fuck that roller coaster. Do you know how much I hate roller coasters in general? I genuinely hate them. Try folding my entire lanky body into a tiny metal box seat. Make sure my hips are pinned between either side real tight, because I have large (some would even say childbearing) hips. Then when my knees are jammed right against the metal box in front of me, violently jerk me around a track until you're absolutely *sure* my week is ruined. Awesome.

When I wasn't actively hating that roller coaster in New York–New York, I kept busy watching Dave, Denny, Sean, and the gang tear it up night after night. Meanwhile, I was limited to acting like Spaulding in *Caddyshack*, finishing everyone's wine. I didn't even *ask* Dave or Sean what went on at night after I went to bed; I was just too incredibly jealous. One of the days they were trying to "take it easy," Dave suggested we go for a walk down the Strip to scope some babes. He bought us both Long Island iced teas (when was the last time you had one of *them*!?). They were thirty dollars each. I drank one thirty-dollar cocktail that came in a whalebone (a.k.a. party yard). That was the extent of my partying in Las Vegas. I took all of that jealous rage and did what every normal healthy teenager should do with their emotions: bury them deep down inside so they could burst out at the seams years later.

Oh, hello, years later. Before my twenty-first birthday even arrived, I made sure I was going to Vegas. I was born in late October, and I was already planning it in August—the year before. It was like my ego and my liver were teaming up to take revenge on that town for how much I'd been stiffed four years prior. They were like Martin Lawrence and Luke Wilson in *Blue Streak,* hilariously scheming up a cockamamie plan that was just headed for trouble. Las Vegas is the perfect way to ring in adulthood, because it is filled with adults acting like children. I was so pent-up, I wanted to go beyond that. I wanted to go 4-D. This trip was just the boyz—Dave, myself, and Sean. Also, my birthday is basically right before Halloween. Having your birthday near a holiday is great, because your birthday will always be celebrated even when no one likes you. Our oldest brother, Sean? He was born on Christmas Day. His birthday is on Christmas every year, and every year he gets double gifts, double booze, and everyone is always partying. If he was born in the middle of August, no one would even know he was born.

Throughout the years, I had gotten my birthday/ Halloween combinaish just right. Skimpy lady costumes, everybody acts silly, then maybe I get a BJ from a treasure troll in a bar bathroom because it's a special occasion (I woke up and my hands, face, and peener were all dyed red from her treasure troll hair coloring). But Halloween in Las Vegas was a completely different story. First off, no one in Vegas gave a shit that it was my birthday. More importantly, have you seen the gals in Vegas? Okay, now, have you seen the gals in Vegas on Halloween?! It's so unbelievable that it's confusing. Las Vegas represents how good-looking the women of Earth have become and just how fucked all of us men are because of it. How did we get here? Has the cosmetic industry come so far with their face creams and moisturizers that women can just constantly shine on with the heat of a thousand suns? Had the fashion industry done a case study on hundreds of sickos like me, somehow gotten into the deepest parts about what makes us tick, and then exploited that with every dress/skirt/tank top a man would ever want to see? At all the right angles?! I find that I am completely powerless around these women.

This was *exactly* what has been going on with gals since the dawn of time. Every century they get hotter and hotter than the last. Every generation they lose a terrible trait of yesteryear (bras in the 1960s? Brutal!) and pick up a cooler, sexier one. Where does the train stop? It was a trend that was all culminating right then, at that moment, as I became a legal adult in Vegas.

Women in Vegas? They're the next stage of evolution. The mutants of sexiness. Women train *all year* for that bachelorette weekend in Vegas. Add *the most promiscuous major holiday* to that equation? We were in over our heads.

In the weeks leading up to the big weekend, we Stangles got to talking. Plans were brewing. Diets had begun. Bets were wagered. Promises were made. Lies were told. Inventory was taken. We needed to go big. We wanted to come up with an original, funny, cheeky, never-done-before costume concept that we could apply to a group. THINK, you guys. THINK HARD. Then procrastinate until it's too late. That's exactly what we did. We got lazy and it didn't happen, so we just went with Tom Cruise's *Risky Business*. High socks, a dress shirt, stupid sunglasses. It's perhaps the most overdone costume in the history of mailing it in. The only thing setting us apart is that three of us were involved. That makes six giant milky-white legs spilling out of tighty whiteys for all of the Las Vegas Strip to deal with. We were pretty much ready to be arrested.

Our first night in Las Vegas had a calm-before-the-storm type of feeling to it. As we got into our costumes the next day, our enthusiasm was next to impossible to contain. We started drinking and scheming much too early. To start—when you buy a pack of Hanes tighty whiteys they come with five pairs. Sean and Dave got to the pack first and got two pairs each and were able to double up while I was left with just one. It was such an advantage, having two pairs of underoos on. First off—I don't know the last time you guys have tried on a pair of tighty whiteys, but they're pretty much see-through. Two pairs fixed that problem. Two pairs also hid any sort of stains or sweat marks that would come from the messy adventure we all knew was ahead. Realizing that advantage, Dave started to call his underwear his "fudgies" and I don't think he's referred to any sort of undergarments, male or female, as anything but "fudgies" since. Second, when you aren't wearing pants, you've got no pockets! Unless you're wearing two pairs of fudgies. In that case, you have an extra fudgie layer in which to tuck away your cell phone, wallet, and some socks to enhance your bulge. With one pair, all this stuff is right up against your private parts. It's just not ideal.

Sean and Dave were walking around fully strapped, fully charged, and with bulges that were tough not to stare at. Their fudgies were stocked. I had to transfer my cell phone and wallet from my coin purse into my high socks, as my fudgies were running the risk of truly becoming fudgy. I felt like I was wearing tissue paper, and I couldn't risk damaging my phone. This would come into play later in the story. If you think it has anything to do with me not having a wallet, cell phone, or any idea where the *fuck* I am, you're absolutely right.

The funny part about having a local Stangle in Las Vegas is we never actually stay on the Strip. We stay at Sean's house off the Strip. It provides so much more room for pregame activities than a hotel room would. Anytime you travel somewhere and you're in a hotel, you go out so much earlier and soberer than you otherwise would, because you don't want to be cooped up in a little hotel room with an expensive minibar glaring at you. When you've got your older brother's terribly decorated raised ranch to party in? Entirely different story. What Sean's house lacked in décor it made up for with a very impressive bar of artisan tequilas. Sean is a big-, *big*-time liquor snob. I mean that in the best and worst ways possible. He can tell you everything you'd never want to know about every kind of liquor. Sure, Sean's furniture was second-rate, his bedding was from Old Navy, and the clothes in his closet belonged on the set of *Melrose Place*. His bar, though? Top-notch. He had spent years researching, hunting down, and collecting rare craft tequilas from around the world. Each bottle was unique and beautiful. It felt like Dave and I were looking into Jay Leno's garage, but instead of classic cars, it was booze.

It was clear he took a lot of pride in his collection, so it was alarming how remorseless Dave and I were when we dug right into it the second he left the house. We were opening four-hundred-dollar bottles of tequila like they were RC Colas, pouring it down each other's throats and chests while Akon (it was 2009!) was blasting in the background. A few of Sean's buddies were at the house with us and could not *believe* what we were doing. Sean seems sort of tough when you don't know him like we do, so I'm guessing no one ever thought to mess with his extravagant liquor collection. When they saw us dive in, those guys went headfirst after us. It was a nice time.

Sean had been out at Target for an hour, getting us our high socks and white fudgies for the night. When he arrived home to discover what we'd done, he was none too pleased. He had that look on his face the dad from *A Christmas Story* has after all those dogs eat his turkey dinner. In the hour he was gone, Dave and I drank over $1,600 worth of tequila. More accurately, we drank about $1,100 and dumped the remaining $500 all over each other. How else were we supposed to feel as sexy as we needed to before we went out? Our first stop of the night was Mandalay Bay. Mandalay is my favorite casino in that entire town. Have you ever seen it? It looks like a solid gold mirror. When you get close to one of the mirrored walls and look at yourself in it, you see what you'd look like if you were made of gold. So you essentially see the perfect you. Sean actually worked there at the time—at a tequila bar (making more sense now?) called the Border Grill. That place is off the hook. It's the best Mexican restaurant you've ever eaten at and they also shove liquor down your throat anytime you aren't inhaling, exhaling, or chewing on some of their world-class ceviche. The Border Grill was a great home base to start at, because it was all people we knew. Good thing, too.

One thing we didn't consider about not wearing pants or shoes in a Las Vegas casino is that Las Vegas casinos require their patrons to wear both pants *and* shoes. Sean's boss at the Border Grill told us we were in for a tough night. He stepped up the "early shots" for us because he thought we'd have a hard time getting served elsewhere. How tough could it actually be, though? Sure, we were walking around in fudgies and high socks, and sure, we looked disgusting, but it was Halloween! Surely everyone would be dressed outrageously. Nope. It was a problem literally *everywhere* we went. Mandalay Bay happens to be on the far west side of the Strip, all the way at the end. As we made our way east from casino to casino, party to party, we were chased out of each new place. Everyone around us was dressed up for Halloween, but we were the ones getting the boot without exception. At least the Luxor had the decency to give us road sodas and let us take the inter-casino tunnels that connect them all. They are lined with the slipperiest carpet you've ever seen in your life—but only if you're just wearing socks. On top of that, Sean had this genius idea when we were getting our costumes ready to tape the bottom of our socks with this white chrome metallic tape his local hardware store yokel told him would give us some extra mileage. No one has ever been more right about anything, ever. The combination of the casino carpet with tight, high socks wrapped in metallic tape was like straight *ice*. We were sliding around that thing like a bunch of maniacs. It was perfect! Tom Cruise's sock slide had never been done so well.

When we were getting escorted out of Excalibur, they had seen what a grand entrance we had made on the ice-carpet and decided to take us out the door instead.

That really stunk, because we had just perfected how to do a fifteen-foot slide on the casino carpets. We were like hockey players who had no place off the ice. All we wanted to do was skate. As I sit here thinking about it, I feel like Forrest Gump on that bench. *Now, you wouldn't believe me if I told you, but I could slide like the wind blows. From that day on, if I was going somewhere, I was sliding!* Walking was out of the picture, we tried to be exclusively sliding whenever possible. Take three steps, slide fifteen. Take another three, slide another fifteen, fall. Get up, get kicked out, slide to the next casino.

We carried on like this not only in the Luxor and Excalibur, but through the Tropicana, New York–New York, and the Monte Carlo. By the time we got to the Monte Carlo, we had our routine down pat. We'd get a running head start toward a bar in the casino, then plant our feet at the entrance to that bar and slide the rest of the way until our hips slammed into either an open spot at the bar or a very angry patron waiting for a drink. Those poor patrons. Imagine if you're waiting at a bar and BOOM a giant guy in his fudgies slams into you and before you can even say anything BOOM there's another, on the other side of you. BOOM! A third just fell directly at your feet and can't get up because he's belly laughing too hard. Do you fight these guys or run for your life? Oh, never mind, security is here to escort them out.

We were very good at getting our drink orders in and paid for before security flagged us each time. This was essential in staying as drunk as we needed to be, considering. The security guards were actually all really nice and had no problem letting us keep our drinks as we were escorted to town lines, just so long as we made our way on the other side of them and became someone else's problem. If you consider the fact that Sean works in hospitality in Vegas, things were pretty bad. He's worked in almost every casino on the Strip at one point or another, and he knows people *everywhere.* On any night before that and any night since, Sean is the darling of Las Vegas. He's got all the credentials. He's from the East Coast, so he at one point had some semblance of a work ethic, he's quick with a joke, and he's a cutie. If you don't believe me, just check out his Facebook profile; he's probably self-confirmed all three compliments via status updates within the last twenty minutes. The guy has a legitimate problem.

At the very least, we had a *solid* buzz going. We did approximately two shots at each casino before we were asked to leave. After the first casino, we learned pretty quickly. Order *immediately* upon dance-sliding into the closest bar in sight. Either order shots or "whiskey neats" when you are eventually denied shots. We'd crush a round real quick, and we'd sit on the next one. We'd act like normal patrons who happened to be wearing only fudgies. We'd act like we didn't have disproportionate leg-to-torso ratios and that our legs had seen the sun at some point, ever. Like clockwork, we'd be asked to leave right after paying for the second round. The real beauty of Las Vegas is that there's no open container law. And no one gives a shit about anything except cheating while you gamble. Since we never gamble, no one gives a shit about us. As long as we had the drinks in our hands, we could take them with us! They didn't even give us to-go cups, they just shooed us out with glasses full of whiskey.

It was early enough that the streets were still full of Halloween people in costume, not just straight-up freaks. Vegas on Halloween is full of freaks, though, so we embraced it and let our freak flags fly a little bit. Dave, Sean, and I grabbed a coupla whalebone Long Island iced teas from a horrified street vendor and took to the strip exactly like three giant *Risky Business* Tom Cruises would have. Sliding, dancing, romancing, all three! People were eating it up, too. Next thing I knew, we were gallivanting around the Strip with a new group of best friends! I wanted to think our new friends were laughing with us, that they thought we were funny and clever and great dancers. Realistically, though, these people just couldn't look away. It was like a car crash.

We decided to take another crack at drinking inside, as people do. Our next stop was the Bellagio. The Bellagio is the queen bee of Las Vegas casinos. For a crew of outlaws, as we were that night, the Bellagio was our Fort Knox. We wanted to approach the Bellagio much like Danny Ocean did in *Ocean's Eleven*. The only problem was, how were we supposed to have unwavering confidence and cheeky gimmicks without our hip black guy speaking cockney English? I know, impossible. All we could do was walk into the Bellagio cautiously and poke around slowly. Okay, not *that* slowly or cautiously. We were still sliding everywhere, just with a little poise, so as not to draw too much attention to ourselves. That was the story with me and Dave, anyway. Sean was so drunk, he was falling every time. He had been so steamed about us drinking all his fancy-pants tequila that he went on an aggressive catch-up campaign and totally overshot his landing. We thought the jig was up until something amazing happened.

Suddenly, like a shooting star, something bright and beautiful and blond slid past us. Dave spotted her first—he always has an eye out for blondes. This beautiful blond streak happened to be a gal with the same costume as us! *Risky Business!* She was inside already and had the whole getup, down to the shades. She wasn't wearing pants or shoes, either. She looked much better in her fudgies than we ever could have hoped for. More than looking great, she was our litmus test. Her mere existence in the Bellagio meant that the Bellagio was fudgie-friendly! No security guards were giving her grief whatsoever. Isn't it fucked-up how much sexism oppresses men?

With the dream-weaver blonde in the *Risky Business* getup leading the way, my brothers and I did our patented dance-slide into the bar and immediately slammed into a large group of Asian people. That didn't go over well. Three giant bouncers saw and were on us in a flash. It was such a flash, in fact, we concluded that they had been warned ahead of time. Las Vegas security apparently is some secret brotherhood, and everybody warns everybody else about troublemakers. We didn't even get a drink at the Bellagio. *WELL, what about the girl version??!!* Sean screamed at the security guy. The bouncer just looked at us like our dad did that time when we tried to pretend the porn on Mom's laptop wasn't our doing. Out we went.

After getting kicked out of so many casinos, we had developed quite the following. We had a posse of people, mostly Asians, taking pictures of us and pointing and yelling. It was like they couldn't believe how much progressively worse we were behaving, the more we got in trouble. What started as a small following soon became a large fan group. Our sheer size and sweatiness combined with our absolutely reckless behavior and inability to stay on our feet made us irresistible. I knew Dave was drunk at this point, because he had no problem with the Asian flash mob following us. He's told me before in confidence that he has a real fear of traveling to Japan, on account of being so much bigger than everyone. He thinks they'll associate him with Godzilla or something. After we got kicked out of the Bellagio, we grabbed another round of outdoor whalebone Long Island iced teas for us and also a bunch for our new group of friends. Big mistake. That tab came to about six hundred dollars, and I'm pretty sure they stopped charging us after they ran out of whalebones. Anything for our new friends, though.

The plan was to walk the Strip east for another half mile, then cross and try our luck at the Hard Rock Café. We adopted a new strategy, in which we chose our next spots based on where Sean was owed the most favors. He was cashing in all his chips that night, and word came to us that the Hard Rock was *actually* fudgie-friendly. It was past midnight at this point, and I was starting to lose steam. I was becoming a mess. I had problems to worry about. While my brothers had their phones and wallets safely tucked between their two pairs of fudgies, I was dealing with a cracked phone and three missing credit cards on account of my stuff repeatedly falling out of my single pair of undies. On top of that, every time I got cash back after buying drinks, I threw it in my undies like it was a big coin purse. It was like I was wearing a diaper made of singles and I legit had a nickel in my butthole. Do you know how dirty money is? Whatever, you only turn twenty-one once, right? I was getting fed up with my phone and wallet getting in the way of my sick-ass dance slides, and I had to be at max flexibility if I was going to keep up with Dave and Sean. Those guys were sliding like the dickens. As a quick and thoughtful solution, I gave my phone and wallet to my new friend Akiha to hold on to. She was dressed up like a sexy cop and had actually let Dave smooch her for a little bit earlier in the night, so I knew I could trust her with my stuff. Asians are trustworthy, right?

You know what aren't trustworthy? Whalebones. Who the fuck drinks cocktails out of those things? They are fucking HUGE! After my last on-the-street whale-bone, well, I blacked out for a while. Maybe it was closer to a brown-out, because I can account for a *few* things. To start, I should not have trusted Akiha. She straight up left and was gone. I had some pretty interesting charges on my cards when I canceled them the next day. Akiha had herself a nice night. When I came to, I was peeing on my feet in a very nice bathroom, and Akiha was probably halfway back to the Orient! I was phoneless, without my wallet, and without brothers in a city where you need that stuff. Where the fuck were they? Where the fuck was I? I grabbed the first trustworthy-looking guy I could find. He was dressed up like James Earl Jones's character in *Coming to America,* the King of Zamunda. He wore a giant lion's head draped over him like a sash and a ton of gold. He nailed that costume, and we hit it off right away. He was very helpful and gave me the facts I needed. I got his number, actually. It's still in my phone under King Jaffe Joffer.

I was at the Hard Rock. Somehow we had gotten in. Or I had gotten in? I wasn't sure if they had been with me or what was really going on. I also didn't have a phone or a wallet, but I did have a drink and my costume was still intact. I was smiling. All good signs. I quickly peeled off one layer of tube socks. Oh, I didn't tell you? I went double tube socks. That was my leverage when my brothers got two pairs of undies and I didn't. With clean socks and a road soda, I set out on the Strip to find my brothers. It couldn't be too difficult, considering the attention we were getting earlier. I took off on my own, having conquered my blackout. The *first* person I asked pointed me toward them. Well, in their general direction, anyway. My hunt quickly became the most entertaining game I've ever played. I kept forgetting how I was dressed and asking people if they'd seen people who were dressed like . . . well, me. It was like following the yellow brick road of giant white guys in their fudgies. I asked every Asian in sight. It was honestly foolproof. *Have you seen two . . . guys who look exactly like me?? Yup! Thatta way. Put some fucking pants on, by the way; you are truly disgusting.* Eventually, I spotted the guys.

How did we have so much energy and how could we continue to drink hard alcohol? Well, it was my twenty-first birthday, so I was automatically invincible. On top of that, we all ate a ton of Adderall during that Akon set from earlier. Have I mentioned how much I sweat? With the combination of Adderall, tequila, dancing, dress shirt with no undershirt, and my fucked-up adrenal glands, it was a rain forest. The circles of sweat under my arms were so big they stretched to my nipples. I can't control it, so I'm not embarrassed about it, okay?! Dave did not let the sweat go unnoticed (as if *anyone* hadn't noticed it already; he just made it okay to talk about). From then on, most of his dance moves were interactive with mine. If I was raising the roof, he was underneath me pretending to wring out my pits like wet washcloths, to the rhythm of the song. He's pretty interpretive.

Put yourself in my shoes for a minute. I'm newly twenty-one, single, my tighty whiteys are well received, and I'm drunk. Remember all that angst about being left out of all the fun last trip to Vegas? That was all forgotten. By now, I was on to looking for love in all the wrong places. What I mean by that is I was being a complete lush. Really *not* playing hard to get. The problem was that every time I was talking to a gal, Dave would walk over at some point with two things: 1) shots, because it was one of those kind of nights; or 2) some sort of insult about my sweaty armpits. The gal would look down, I'd act weird, she'd walk away. Dave would be satisfied, we'd take the shots. I didn't mind at first. Things repeated like that for a while, until I started to get really drunk-mad.

As we were cruising toward the eastern side of the Strip, I ran around the corner, determined to dupe Dave somehow. I needed to embarrass him, hit him with something, just *get him*. I came across a stack of newspapers that were advertising nudie gals. It was bundled up pretty good. Immediately my brain replayed a cartoon I once saw of Bugs Bunny smacking some guy with a stack of newspapers. Hilarious. That is exactly what I would do. The Asians will *love this*. I bent down to grab the papers, just as Dave was coming around the corner toward me yelling, "Where are you, you Sweaty Sack of Shit!?" I executed your classic spinning shot-put throw and absolutely crushed Dave with the stack of papers, right off his feet. Hilarious! Well, until he didn't get up. A cool fourteen seconds later, one of our new friends whipped out some smelling salts. Why was this guy carrying smelling salts? I don't know. The real question is, why don't *you* carry smelling salts? They can come in handy. I now carry smelling salts, in fact.

Dave came to immediately, and I stopped nervous sweating, but continued regular sweating. He was okay, kind of. Something had changed. The first thing I expected to happen was for him to attack me physically. I had really gotten him good with the stack of papers, much worse than I saw it playing out in my head. Fortunately, he was concussed to the point of retardation. He didn't remember what I'd done to him, thank God. I quickly blamed it on my least favorite Asian in the group, and we carried on. On top of the unhealthy amount of drugs and alcohol that were in his system, his brain was now functioning in four-wheel low. He was on all fours, crawling slowly, for a long time. I could not believe the things he was forgetting. We can laugh about it now, because he's still here and only a little slower than he used to be, but at the time, Sean and I were downright worried.

The rest of the night, Dave made no sense whatsoever. He kept wandering off the Strip with groups that were not ours. We did a pretty good job of keeping concussed Dave with us and without a beverage in his hand for the rest of the night, until the very end of it. Our Asian posse was very concerned with his well-being and helped us keep him out of trouble. Those guys were good to him, but they called it a night around three and the Stangle boys were alone once more. Around 4 a.m., things were getting hazy again. All I can really say is that at some point, Sean and I lost Dave. Flat-out lost him. In our defense, holding on to Dave was like trying to keep track of a learning-disabled dog with amnesia. He didn't even recognize us at that point. What about long-term brain damage, you say? That's not the point of the story, so quit asking questions. Dave and I will hash that out between us.

Sean was in the middle of explaining the finer points of a rare tequila he insisted we drink, out of our minds, at four in the morning, when I realized we lost Dave. Shit. The brother search was on again. Sean and I were incredibly inefficient in our search. The *have you seen a guy dressed like us?* line was no longer working. I think this was because we were so drunk none of the words came out like that, and we were also really beat up and dirty from the marathon party that was coming to a close. Blood, sweat, and fudgies. No one would help us. After another whalebone Long Island iced tea and a full lap of the entire Strip, we had been looking for two hours and hadn't seen him in at least three.

We stopped in front of Treasure Island, defeated. If you've never been there, a giant pirate ship sits right out front in some water that resembles a lagoon. I was leaning on a railing, looking at the pirate ship, and my peripheral vision caught Dave. He was wading aimlessly through the thigh-deep water. He did not look good, and he was walking exactly like a zombie. We flagged him down and got him out of the water, and were happy to have found him. He explained to us that he'd just been taking a quick swamp nap on the side of the pirate ship display and there was nothing to worry about. He had probably swallowed a little water, sure, but he needed to hydrate anyway, he explained. He couldn't explain where he'd been or what he'd been doing for the past three hours; he just kept repeating "swamp nap" in this weird little kid voice. We stopped asking questions and conceded to getting a room at Treasure Island for the night. We woke up three across a full-sized bed and had no complaints. We were alive.

Since Dave'd had his swamp nap, he naturally had the most energy the next morning. He did some research and attempted to piece together our night. Remember, this was 2009, so hashtags were in their awkward teenage years. It didn't matter, we were *all over* the Internet. Sliding, dancing, kissing, puking, full frontal nudity, you name it. Facebook, Twitter, Photobucket, Myspace, fucking Webshots.

As many times as we've recounted that story, I always manage to evade blame for severely concussing Dave with the newspapers. In fact, I have made the ultimate sacrifice in writing this, because he *still* has no idea it was me. When he reads this for the first time in a couple of minutes, he is not going to be the happiest guy.

Afterword

We Fed Mom a Pot Cookie

Mama,

That wasn't so bad, was it? Oh, you aren't even reading anymore, because you're sobbing uncontrollably? Thanks for still loving us. We're published now. That means we'll get to go to some after-parties that go on after the parties we'll get to go to. There will be champagne everywhere. Do you want to come? Let us first just check that we aren't getting authors confused with rappers, and then we'll send you all the details.

Listen, while we've got you here and we're all on the nonjudgment train, we'd like to get one last thing off our chests. We are genuinely sorry you're finding out about this now, and I'm sure the night in question will now make a lot more sense, but it was *really* funny. Besides, if we know you like we think we do—you'll be laughing and shaking your head any minute now.

Remember when you and Dave came out to visit me in Colorado in the winter of 2012? We skied, we partied, we hit the hot springs, we laughed. Remember that first night, how particularly hard we laughed? We laughed so hard, it didn't even make sense. We can probably make some sense of it now.

You know those times when you're put in a situation and you realize that the right thing to do, the responsible thing to do, and the decent thing to do are all the same thing? Then you shrug, look at your brother for confirmation, and do the exact opposite? Dave is a master of that situation—such a dick. I still can't understand why he's your favorite.

Anyway, Mama, I'll cut to the chase. It was Colorado and I was twenty-two years old, so naturally I had a ton of pot stuff around the house. You saw it, thanks for not judging. You, me, Dave, Sean, and about eight of my close friends were sitting in my living room having a few cocktails around the fire after a nice day on the slopes. It was getting late, the wine was flowing. Denny, you were a little buzzed—don't worry, we peer-pressured you. I looked over and there's Dave with a big ol' pot cookie in hand. Yes, Mama, that cookie had pot in it. It all happened too fast!

You: Oh, Dave! I didn't know we had dessert.
       Where'd you get that, it looks delicious?

One second of hesitation. Dave and I look at each other, shrug.

Dave: Take it, I'm getting fat anyway.

You: Thanks, Dave, this is DELICIOUS.

Next thing I know, you're mowing down the magical treat. Giggles ensue. You even asked me for the recipe! Don't worry, there's no way Dad made it far enough through the book to actually read this. That night is going to make a lot more sense to you now, huh? Sorry, mama! Love you!

Dave and Mike

Mike, Dave, and Dave's forehead as kids. Not pictured: The fucking genius who designed Mike's outfit.

Appendix

*Craigslist as a Creative Outlet
to Sell Everything!*

Shitty End Table

For sale is this here end table. Some call it a bed-side table. It is a cool color green and very stur-dy and in good shape. My ex-girlfriend sanded it, painted it for me, put new handles on it, then promptly dumped me. If bought for full price, top drawer will come with a nudy shot of her inside of it (8x 10, framed for an extra $10). It is two drawer and good for socks, underwear, other unspeakables. Bulldog not automatically includ-ed (negotiable), only shown for size comparison.

It's NOT ok to contact this poster with services or other commercial interests.

Posting ID: 3546505915
Posted: 2013-01-14, 9:39PM EST

On Mon, Jan 14, 2013, at 10:06 PM, Beth Babicz (bethbabicz@xxxxxx.com) wrote:
Hi there,

I'm very interested in the end table. What are the dimen-sions? I'd be able to come by and pick it up tomorrow night if that works for you.

Also, I'd be glad to take the bulldog off your hands!

Please let me know.

Thanks!

Beth

On Jan 14, 2013, at 10:11 PM, Dave Stangle (dave. stangle@xxxxxx.com) wrote:
Hi Beth,

Tomorrow works. The dimensions are: 14 inches deep, 17.5 wide, 22 inches high. The bulldog is currently passed out next to me snoring very loudly. Should he keep it up I will consider giving him up to you upon your arrival.

On Mon, Jan 14, 2013, at 10:58 PM, Beth Babicz (bethbabicz@xxxxxx.com) wrote:
Sounds good. I work in upper east until 8:30, so would 8:45 be ok?

I'll keep my fingers crossed for the pup.

Sent from my iPhone

On Tue, Jan 15, 2013, at 10:42 PM, Beth Babicz (beth-babicz@xxxxxx.com) wrote:
Hey Dave,

So I love my end table but I have to admit—my room-mates were pretty disappointed that I didn't make friends with the funny craigslist guy. We do feel that we are just as witty, so if you're ever interested in playing Apples to Apples here's my number: 9413213XXX.

Beth
Sent from my iPhone

From: Dave Stangle (dave.stangle@xxxxxx.com)
Date: Wed, Jan 16, 2013, at 9:06 PM
Subject: Re: Cool green end table—$34
(Upper East Side)
To: Beth Babicz (bethbabicz@xxxxxx.com)
Cc: anthony@xxxxxx.biz, Timothy Clinton
(Timothy.M.Clinton@xxxxxx.com), Howard
Freedman (howard.d.freedman@xxxxxx.com),
Jackson Kiniry (jackson.kiniry@xxxxxx.com)
Beth,

I apologize for a lack of small talk last night when you purchased the end table I advertised on craigslist. By the time you came to the door a combination of work related stress and severe back pain (from my bad boy lifestyle $$$) had driven me deep into a drug and alcohol fueled haze by which my manners completely escaped me. Had there been less chemicals in my blood stream, which is the case *most* Tuesdays, I would have offered you a chilled glass of box wine while we spoke of end tables, bulldogs, and your recent move to Manhattan's East Village. I would also like to apologize as my ad on craigslist clearly states that any buyer who pays full price for the end table is entitled to a nudy shot of my ex-girlfriend. I will consider this an open case. A Lannister always pays his debts.

Regarding your invitation to play Apples to Apples—I happily accept on the grounds that you agree to the following: Everyone knows Apples to Apples is a game based not only on speed, wit, panic, passion, and facetiousness . . . but also on sheer numbers. A game of A2A played 1 vs. 1 would just be downright silly (and at this point creepy as we already owe knowing each other to a craigslist ad). Copied on this email are 4 men. I know each of these men well and can attest to that fact that each of them meets at least 3 of the following 5 characteristics:

1. Tall
2. Single
3. Free Spirited
4. Between moderately to extremely handsome.
5. A 3-time convicted felon wanted in several states and banned for life from all of South America (under the penalty of death in Bolivia).

Although I am yet to even mention this to any of the 4 men copied (this is the first they are hearing of this) I am confident they will be up for a good game of A2A, however, will require you to counter with a similar group of young

women. I keep a detailed dossier on each of the men cop-
ied and can provide brief biographies upon request.

Dave Stangle

(no response whatsoever)

Personal Trainer

Innovative personal trainer for overweight
women. (NYC)

Are you an over weight woman looking to
trim down? I have an adrenaline pumping and
intense exercise routine that just may interest
you! What I offer is a cross training service to
help you slim down, improve your cardiovas-
cular activity, and have some fun! Here is how
it works!

We meet at a specific outdoor location of my
choosing with a decent amount of stairs, side-
walks, crosswalks, buildings, etc in NYC. I'll
give you a head start of about 30 seconds then I
come chase you down like a raging lunatic! I'm
6'4" and whiter than snow. Picture Silas from The
Da Vinci Code—fucking terrifying. I also have
an uncontrollable drinking problem so you'll

know I'll have incredibly blood shot eyes and smell like I slept in the basement of a gin distillery! Aside from my general appearance and lack of emotional stability I have several other tactics to make you want to run away from me and raise your heart rate in a fun and exciting way!

Worried about being in too poor a shape to participate? Don't worry! I've got all the bases covered. When I start to close in on some of my fatter slower clients I yell nonsensical words and racial slurs while holding my hands out like a zombie!! I've found it really lights a fire under their butts. If I do catch you prior to the conclusion of the workout I'll simply bite your ankles several times until you kick your way free and hit the home stretch for a solid finish!

So if you are interested in getting in shape and having some good old fashioned fun while doing it, please, just email me! I am available most weekends and some week nights. Prices are negotiable. Summer is right around the corner, ladies!

Location: NYC

It's NOT ok to contact this poster with services or other commercial interests.

License info: Unlicensed

Posting ID: 1722663588
Posted: 2010-05-03, 3:24PM EDT

Bear Taxidermy

RE: Giant Bear Taxidermy

Hi -

This bear is the coolest thing I've ever seen. Seriously. Have you sold it yet?

I see you are selling it for $729. Unfortunately, we are in a large recession and I cannot afford it. I propose a counter offer. What if you were to GIVE my room mates and I Chester (I've already named him) for free and we will re-pay you by hunting down and killing an even larger animal next chance we get. Weapons, no weapons. Your choice.

Think about it..

(no response)

RE: Giant Bear Taxidermy (the truth)

Alright, I'm rolling up the sleeves. It's time you hear the truth about this Bear you are selling.

I killed that big motherfucker with my own bare hands (pun! aayyooo!) and left in-sizer tooth. I'd recognize it anywhere. I tried to barter, I tried to offer counter proposals. I didn't want to tell you this, but the truth is inevitable. I killed that fucking bear, therefore I am the rightful owner of it's stuffed half carcass. I don't know who you bought it off of for "$2500" in the underground taxidermy black market, but clearly this vendor has forgotten the great lesson taught to us by Keith David in the 1990 classic film Men At Work, that is, "Never touch anotha' mans fries." It's time you hear the truth.

It was the winter of 1979, the coldest winter on record as I'm sure you remember. The middle east was once again playing hardball with Jimbo Carter and oil prices were through the roof. My modest 1 bedroom cabin upstate was burning on what little oil it had left. I had calculated I had about 4 hours of heat left before finding an additional source, but I wasn't going to wait around to find out. I set out into the forest with nothing but my knife, my boots, and my rapist wit. My goal was to hunt chipmunks, house cats, and other varmint of similar nature. soon I found much more than I bargained for. After about 6pm I stumbled upon "your" bear, Chester, smack dab in the middle of the woods taking a shit (yes, the legends are true). I snuck up from behind him, knife drawn, with hopes of slitting his throat. When I was about 8 feet away I accidental stepped on a dry twig which made a "snap" sound. He twirled around and threw a ninja star at me, dislodging my knife from my hand. It was clear this was going to come down to fisticuffs. It was on. We exchanged blows for the better part of a day and a half, right there in the middle of the woods. The next part gets a little blurry as I had lost well over 2 quarts of blood, but when my memory came to I was laying on Chesters dead body, my tooth had ripped him square across the chest and spilled his insides all over the cold ground and my face. It was only then I realized the harsh truth. Chester was pregnant, there were 4 little bear cubs that spilled out of his stomach. I was mortified. I made a pact right there that Chester's last battle would not be in vain. I immediately had his carcass stuffed to be preserved and began nursing the 4 cubs on my teet. Days turned into weeks, weeks into months, and months into years. I put each of those 4 bears through college (2 of which have made the dean's list in consecutive semesters). Now with Brett, the youngest of the 4 in his senior year, I looked into tracking down Chester to return him to his rightful home. I have traveled all over the world looking for this carcass, and my search has lead to to craigslist. To you.

Hear me now. Arrange a meeting to exchange what is rightfully mine and I promise I will protect you from all future Bear attacks. If you refuse, and word gets out in the wildlife community what you are harboring from me. well I'm sorry my friend. You are on your own.

(no response)